Area

of

Service

Written by Darold Edwards

Copyright © 2008 Darold F. Edwards
Editing Assistance by MyKeyWeb.com

Area of Service

Table of Contents:

i.	Introduction	5
ii.	Acknowledgements	15
iii.	Preface	19
I.	Area of Service	25
II.	Coming Out	43
III.	Imposed Impulses	65
IV.	Judgments	81
V.	Born or Created	99
VI.	Benefits and Rewards	105
VII.	Innocence	119
VIII.	Before Coffee Thoughts	137

NOTES

i.

A General Introduction to
The Works of
Darold Edwards

I would like to begin this introduction of myself and my writings with a greeting to all who are gracious enough to take the time to read my writings and join me in this journey of Bible exploration and study. This greeting is found in **[2 Peter 1: 2], "Grace and peace be multiplied to you through the knowledge of God, and of Jesus our Lord". In [Galatians 2: 6] Paul writes of people "who added nothing to me".** It is my desire and prayer that these writings will add much to you in your Bible explorations and enrichment of life.

Let me introduce myself to you. It is very likely you have never heard of me but that is alright, as I have never heard of the vast majority of you, but, I know you are out there somewhere in our big wide world that seems to be getting smaller with a disturbing amount of consistency. At the present time I am 75 years old, and like most of everything else in this world, my age is subject to constant change. My wife of 52, going on 53years of marriage, Patricia, is a very wonderful person who has had the grace to put up with me these many years gone by and has been a constant source of help, strength, and encouragement to me; with a little challenge thrown in from time to time to help keep life interesting. But having no complaints, I am looking forward to a continuation of our life together, at least for some time to come. We have our home in Albany, Oregon, raised 3 children there and have grandchildren and great grandchildren.

After a privileged time as a child and young person under the care and guidance of some very wonderful loving parents, I proceeded on to adulthood with an average course of life doing some things I should and some that I shouldn't. My specific vocation, after various jobs, was about 42 years as an electrician which was enjoyed very much. In the latter portion of this time I was able and blessed to assist in many church construction jobs as an electrician. There came a time, however, that my body convinced me it was time to seek other easier things to do. After that career ran its course and was fading into the sunset, I was led into an interest in writing, which is where I am today and will probably be for the remainder of my time on this earth. I am enjoying it with much satisfaction, and what you see here is among the beginnings of it. I hope you will blessed by it.

My main interest and priority is and has been in pursuit of Biblical study and knowledge for several years. As I get an ever increasing **"Vision of the Value"** of such study and exploration, the interest and priority increases accordingly. This Biblical knowledge with its provision of life and life more abundantly through Jesus Christ our Lord, indeed has become my life with its great and perfect peace with joy unspeakable and full of glory. What a blessed state of being to enjoy an unending hope and blessed assurance of a future that extends from today on to and including eternity.

Not being very impressed with humanity in its general condition and what it has done to this world God has provided for it, much of my writings will be addressing this issue and whose responsible for such a degraded condition as this world is in, including our "Land of the Free and the Home of the Brave". You may not agree with me in some of my views and interpretations, but it is only important that you be in agreement with Jesus. Some of the positions I take on traditional Bible interpretations will be somewhat controversial, maybe even viewed as heretical by some, but will certainly provide reason for some new exploration of thinking and thought. God tells us in **[Isaiah 55: 8-9], "My thoughts are not your thoughts,** neither are my ways your ways, saith the Lord. For as the heavens are higher than the earth, so are my ways higher than your ways, and my thoughts than your thoughts".

So as we re-explore some of these old traditional truths and absolutes of God's Word that have brought life, strength, stability, and comfort to all who embrace them, lets keep our minds open to other additional concepts, original ideas, thoughts and ways that are a part of the expanse between where we are today and where God is calling us to be. I do not believe, that in the fullness of God's greatness, man has reached the end of all God has for us to think about either in the knowledge we are to gain or in the development of our mental capabilities. Much education and knowledge lay before us yet to be attained to. Once again, it is not important that you agree with me, but don't get caught in disagreement with God and his Word, that is a fatal mistake that is much to prevalent in our world today.

My writings are not meant to be entertaining, though a bit of mirth from time to time is acceptable. Yet encouragement and inspiration for meditation and diligent, committed study for spiritual growth and development resulting in intimate fellowship and relationship with God and our Saviour and Lord Jesus Christ is, and remains, the priority. I will be using some words that may offend some but are meant to describe some very apparent conditions that are alive, but are more sick than well, yet thriving and somewhat destructive, in humanity. God is much more of a gentleman than I am and limits his language to words such as fool, fools, and foolishness. I get a little rougher in my references to mankind and use words such as stupid, idiotic, ignorance etc.

Please understand I have nothing against people, only against the conditions listed above, stupidity, idiocy, and ignorance, etc, that humanity has such an overwhelming desire to wallow and remain in to the degradation of themselves, their societies, and nations, when God, in his love, has given us the remedy for deliverance from such nonsense. To refuse, or neglect, to avail oneself of what God has made available for deliverance from sin and its results in itself, puts a persons intelligence in question.

You are certainly welcome to disagree with me and raise an argument in protest if you wish, however, just a little understanding of the condition our nation is in and how it arrived at this state of demise from the abominations of sin and iniquity of its inhabitants should settle the argument and any questions about it once and for all.

I do hope to wake many minds that have gone to sleep to the challenge of some new in-depth thought that will project them into new ways of life and living where **"the heart is diligently kept, clean, and guarded" [Proverbs 4:23], the mind and spirit are renewed, [Romans 12: 2; Psalms 51:10], and the soul prospers" [3 John: 2].** If we continue to think the way we've always thought, we'll continue to get what we've always got. The way humanity is digressing, we cannot afford to continue along that road of demented mentality, either as individuals or as a nation.

It is my intention that other books will be written as the inspiration to do so presents itself. Several others are already in the works, all dealing with Biblical truths as they relate to the problems and dilemmas of our present day and time; all based on man's disobedience and rebellion against God. This has been the story down through the ages and has only intensified as the population of man has increased, **[Hosea 4: 7], "As they were increased, so they sinned against me: therefore I will change their glory into shame"**. It is this increase in intensity of disobedience, rebellion, sin, iniquity, etc, etc, call it what you will, that has proven so disastrous to mankind that prompts referral to the conditions of stupidity, idiocy, and ignorance with which man has so chosen to characterize himself.

It is the overabundance of these things that has brought such confusion and chaos to our nation and indeed the world. We could work our way through some of it, but when it became the norm of mankind's mentality and conduct, we have become overwhelmed by it, and can no longer see a light at the end of the tunnel, so to speak. The problems have not changed thru the ages, but remain internal, in the mentalities of some of **"our own countrymen"** who have formed alliances against the Bible, its teachings, and those who teach it. As a result, our leaders are frustrated, the news media is frustrated, and consequently the people are driven to frustration, and confusion seems to reign supreme, especially in the ranks of the people who have rejected God's word of truth and absolutes.

I will refrain from opening any argument as to whether or not the redeemed community of Christ are any better than the unsaved, as **[John 3: 16]** points out that Christ died for all, of which we were all qualified as ungodly, **[Romans 3: 23], " For all have sinned and come short of the glory of God"**. I am willing to leave that distinction between the saved and unsaved up to God as he separates the sheep from the goats, as who qualifies as a sheep versus a goat is entirely up to him, **[Matthew 25: 32]**. In the meantime, however we might consider **[Acts 10: 34-35]** as a point of interest and consideration by those who have eyes to see, ears to hear, and minds that are capable of comprehension and at least a little bit of understanding; **"Then Peter open his mouth and said, of a truth I perceive that God is no respecter of persons: BUT in every nation he that feareth him, and worketh righteousness, is accepted with him"**.

Having favor with God through meeting his Biblical directed requirements for such favor, and being accepted with him is a very comforting, and intelligent, position to be in. You may well get away with disagreeing with me, but to disagree with God will have some eternal devastating affects: I would suggest a path more in line with God's choosing. I would offer **[Deuteronomy 30: 19]** for intense consideration and study for beginners and as a refresher for the more advanced students, or just readers, of the Bible.

Please don't get me wrong: I am not down on America, only the stupidity and ignorance that is bringing about her ruin, and the idiots that promote and practice it; which is all within their "rights" of course. God created us to be intelligent beings, however, Adam cast that aside when he abdicated his dominion authority to Satan in the Garden of Eden, and man has been abdicating every since. Retained and exercised Godly intelligence would prevent the things that are bringing ruination, shame, and disgrace on our beloved America, but Godly intelligence and common sense seem to be non-existent in our nation these days along with other things mentioned in the Bible that are commensurate with righteous and holiness.

The question of, who is to blame, should prompt some interesting discussion and dialogue. Who knows, during the process, we might even discover the solution to many of our problems. As Christians, that should already be quite apparent. **[Isaiah 5: 24], "Therefore as the fire devoureth the stubble, and the flame consumeth the chaff, so their root shall be as rottenness, and their flower shall go up as the dust: BECAUSE they have cast away the law of the Lord of hosts, and despised the word of the Holy One of Israel".** The first portion of this scripture gives us a fair description of America if we don't get our spiritual act together. The latter portion gives us the result of excommunicating God and His Word by such things as "the separation of the church and state".

Then we have the remedy, **[Mark 1: 15], "Repent and believe the gospel unto diligent obedience.** This is a repeat of **[2 Chronicles 7: 14], "If my people, which are called by my name, shall humble themselves, and pray, and seek my face, and turn from their wicked ways;** *then* **I will hear from heaven, and will forgive their sin, and will heal their land".** There are a few more words used to emphasize this repentance essential, but the message is the same. **[Deuteronomy 28]** gives a very graphic difference between the people who dwell on the **"If thou wilt hearken diligently"** side of God's directions versus the unrepentant, **"If thou wilt not hearken diligently"** side in rebellion and disobedience. Consider this carefully.

Lacking the extended education that many of today's authors have, you may find my writings a bit rough around the edges for which I make no apology. This could prove an advantage in some ways as I don't have some things to unlearn as I progress and move ahead in my own studies. However, if we all stay with the same Bible for the purpose of unity, **[John 17]**, and, to put in today's vernacular, "being on the same page", worshipping and serving the same God, creator of heaven and earth, the God of Israel, and diligently adhering to His counsel, we should remain fairly accurate as we progress, **"seated together in heavenly places in Christ"**, **[Ephesians 2: 4-10]**, continuing toward our eternal destiny of the kingdom of heaven while **[Deuteronomy 28: 47], "serving the Lord our God with joyfulness, and with gladness of heart for the abundance of all things"**.

Though it seems that I may ramble a bit from time to time, it is my intention, whether I succeed or not, to present the readers with some Biblical truths and challenges they can get their "spiritual teeth into" for the purpose of growth, and development that they can apply toward Christian maturity, providing they are interested in doing so. If they are not so inclined, it is my prayer that some of these writings will induce enough curiosity to provide a challenge to compel them to additional studies, with my own writings and a multitude of others that are available to them. Let me challenge you to choose the books you read, and study, with wisdom and discretion, selecting only those that **"add something to you"** in the way of developing a Biblical, Christ like character, personality and attitude, **"with the Word of God dwelling in you richly"**, **[Colossians 3: 15-17], vs. 16.**

You may find an occasional word misspelled for which I do apologize. Nevertheless, my main concern is that it is not misspelled so badly that it fails to contribute constructively to the message it is intended to convey. Allow me to assume my readers will have enough grace to overlook my errors and enough intelligence to get over the rough spots and around the chuck holes and capture the essence of these writings. May God richly bless you as you graciously walk with me through my efforts to present God's truth and absolutes to you for counsel, guidance, and direction unto life and life more abundantly, giving glory, honor, and pleasure, to God, magnifying our Saviour Jesus, and edifying the body of Christ.

Although I am a fan of the Kings James Version, which I will use in the majority of my writing, I will not hesitate to refer to other Versions from time to time as occasionally I will find a word or phrase that seems more preferable to what needs to be said in order to get a better understanding of the message being given. An attempt will be made to identify the use of these various scriptures from the different versions with an explanation of why they are being used in preference to the

K.J.V. By doing this it is hoped we can "stay on the same page".

You will notice the use of much scripture throughout my writing with several scriptures being used many times in various situations. You may criticize this as redundancy if you wish. We were all born critics and man has developed it to a fine art, whether it be constructive or destructive, which it is in most cases as man has only to allow his nature to take its natural course to do this. However, what some may view as redundancy in the often use and application of Biblical truths, I simply see as **"emphasis"** to be diligently applied as needed substance for Christian character and development in all our lives. May God give you additional understanding of his word every time you come into contact with it. May it be often and consistent; for emphasis and effect, of course.

As a conclusion to this introduction, allow me once again to go to the scriptures, **[Hebrews 13: 20-21], "Now the God of peace, that brought again from the dead our Lord Jesus, that great shepherd of the sheep, through the everlasting covenant, Make you perfect in every good work to do his will, working in you that which is well pleasing in his sight, through Jesus Christ; to whom be glory for ever and ever. Amen.** I look forward to meeting you in heaven, and possibly before.

Sincerely, in God's love
Darold F. Edwards

NOTES

ACKNOWLEDGMENTS

I would like to thank the people who from the very beginning as a novice writer were kind enough to read some of my earliest efforts and gave me some very encouraging reviews. First of course I would like to thank God for guiding me into writing. It has become a real Godsend to me and has provided direction and purpose for me at a time when otherwise, retirement could have been very trying. I need purpose in my life and writing of the nature you will see in these books gave me that. During my electrical career when I was able to help build some material churches, I thought that someday I would like to assist in building the spiritual church in the hearts and lives of people. God has opened the door to do that through writing for which I wish to express my soul depth gratitude.

Next, many heartfelt thanks to my dear wife Pat for encouraging me in everything along the way in our life together, what a strength and help she has been to me. Susan Canfield was one of the first, who has been very encouraging from the start. She also trims our Schnauzer, Max, which is another big help. This doesn't really have anything to do with my writing except it provides opportunity to visit with Susan from time to time to get additional input on the writing; she is always encouraging. Susan has been very helpful and encouraging in her comments and friendship. Thank you Susan.

Then there is Jock and Karen Elliot, some dear Christian friends who along with their family we have been blessed to know for many reasons including their encouragement in writing. Karen is also a great cook, which is another real advantage to knowing the right people, and I have been much blessed in this area by her talent. My son Myke is of an absolute necessity and blessing as he is my computer expert along with being my son and a very dear friend. I couldn't do this without him. Thanks Myke, for your ever patient and loving assistance along the way.

Then there is my dear friend and brother in the Lord, Clarence Parker, who comes over a couple of times a week just to talk, discuss, study Bible, and add his encouragement to me in my writing efforts. His comments are extremely uplifting and helpful. He also benefits from Karen's cooking, as do all who attend the Elliot's prayer meetings. What a great blessing and strength he is. Thank you my brother for standing alongside me during my writing struggles. Another dear friend, Nancy Gerling, has read some of my writings and has copies of my first efforts to have books published. She has always been extremely uplifting with her input concerning my writing. Many thanks to you, Nancy.

There are others that have added much to me with their encouraging comments about my works which are much appreciated. May God's blessings be upon them and may his presence fill their hearts and lives. May God's blessings also be added to you who are gracious enough to become a part of my reading public; let us study God's word together as he quickens us together in Christ, raises us up together, and makes us to sit together in heavenly places in Christ Jesus our Lord and Saviour, these places being made heavenly because of His presence, wherever that may be. May God's divine love abound in our hearts toward one another. Indeed; we do become a part of each other as we are a part of the body of Christ our Lord.

A little over a year ago as I was looking through a magazine advertising for a Restore America event, I run across another page where someone made the statement, **"How much**

information do we need before we get out of the boat and walk on the water". Whoever that person is, and wherever he may be, I would like to thank him for impacting my life with that inspirational word. Stepping out in faith and writing as I feel led of the Lord in my efforts is my way of walking on the water.

Your efforts are probably of a different calling than mine, but yet of the divine nature. May we blend our efforts and lives together in the unity Jesus prayed for in **John 17** for God's glory, honor, and pleasure. Come, walk with me as we journey along together with the multitudes who will join with us, as we all walk and sit together **"in heavenly places"**, inspiring each other as Jesus inspires us all. **To God be the glory forever and ever, Amen.**

NOTES

PREFACE

[Ecclesiastes 12: 11-12], "The words of the wise are as goads, and as nails fastened by the masters of the assemblies, which are given from one Shepard. And further, by these, my son, be admonished: of making many books there is no end; and much study is a weariness to the flesh". Much study demands considerable self discipline, diligence and determination, and a lot of invested time, whereas simply reading for the enjoyment of what is being read, or other lesser purposes, without the element of **"study to show thyself approved unto God", [2 Timothy 2: 15],** tends to a great waste of time.

However, such is not the case if a time of relaxation from business or other things that tend to stress is needed, and reading a good book that is a "no brainer" may be just the ticket. Unfortunately this becomes the norm for many people. As a result many books that neither contribute anything of value and add nothing constructive to the readers, are in great abundance, and offer no challenge for growth and development. Consequently no study is required that would demand thought and concentration, so these books are read in pursuit of nothing, then put aside in favor of another "nothing" book or maybe just watching soap operas on T.V. or the equivalent in "nothing". Habits are thus formed with the result being wasted time and life.

Allow me to express extreme caution in the selection of your reading material as your reading is a direct input into the content of your mind and contributes heavily to "the abundance of your heart". So once again I say, proceed with wisdom, knowledge, understanding, and caution, applying some intelligence and plain common sense along the way, **[Proverbs 4: 23], "Keeping thy heart with all diligence; for out of it are the issues of life". [Proverbs 2: 11], "Discretion shall preserve thee; understanding shall keep thee".**

If we do not endeavor to establish our values and standards according to God's values and standards, we will exist in error continually without the life God has made available to us through Jesus Christ. It is with this in mind that I have set out to produce this work concerning the "RESURRECTION OF EXCELLENCY", to challenge the readers, whoever or wherever they may be: to look inside themselves and ask intelligent questions about their being, who they are, what they are, how they came to be, their purpose, and what their eternal destiny is, and what it is comprised of and by God's design. I find it very enlightening to realize I have by "intelligent design" been created as a very special and unique being instead as a blob of something left to chance as claimed by some who are also willing to risk their eternal destiny with their continuing low level of an unchallenged demented mentality.

Don't think me uncaring and insensitive to others because I use words such as stupidity, idiocy, and ignorant at times. We have all been there and if we are not careful and conscientious about our Christian training, have a tendency to revert back to old habits from time to time. I have nothing against man; only against the inadequate mentalities they have chosen to victimize themselves with. Even as Christians, former erroneous habits and desires, at times even with God's assistance, are hard to shake and it takes time, perseverance and diligence to cast them aside and grow out of them. They may or may not be classified as sin in all cases, but regardless consist of things that do not **"please the Lord," [John 8: 29]**, or **"accompany salvation," [Hebrews 6: 9]**. But in any event we need to **[2 Timothy 2: 15], "Study to show ourselves approved unto God, workmen** that needeth not to be ashamed, rightly dividing the word of truth." This involves the extensive effort of **[Romans 12: 2] "being transformed by the renewing of the mind", "exercising thyself unto Godliness", [1 Timothy 4: 7].**

The displacing of these life destroying discrepancies will only be accomplished with the diligent study and input of God's Word. These are just simply some destructive traits of humanity that if not addressed and dealt with according to God's counsel, will continue to plague their unsuspecting, unknowledgeable victims regardless of whether or not they are saved. The devil is not choosey who he victimizes and he will use any method at his disposal to re-devour anyone who becomes negligent in the **"keeping of the heart with all diligence", [Proverbs 4: 23]**. Remember, as a Christian, you are his prime target, you are his priority. All others are already devoured. Such is the result of disregarding God's counsel and direction to **"choose life and blessing rather than death and cursing" [Deuteronomy 30: 19].**

I have had to reject the traditional terminology of "sinner saved by grace" in favor of **"a new creature in Christ, saved by Grace", [2 Corinthians 5: 17].** The reason for this was because the term "sinner" was not conducive to being **[1 John 1: 7-9], "forgiven of sin and cleansed from all unrighteousness by the blood of Jesus."** This is an insult to the power of the blood of Jesus to thoroughly cleanse from sin and unrighteousness in the name of Jesus for complete cleansing, forgiveness, deliverance and reconciliation. All this of course, is based on the condition of genuine, soul depth, repentance of sin and a commitment to **"fear [reverence] the Lord and work righteousness" [Acts 10: 35], serving the Lord with joyfulness and with gladness of heart, for the abundance of all things, [Deuteronomy 28: 47].** You may not agree with me on this issue and that's not important. Just be in agreement with God. It's his word that counts, not mine.

After all that God has done for us through Jesus Christ our Lord and Saviour in obtaining the **"divine nature of God through his great and precious promises", [2 Peter 1:2 -4],** it seemed that the title and name of "sinner" had some rather antagonistic and invasive qualities and connotations about it that never belonged nor fit in well with being "a new creature in Christ saved by grace". The term "sinner" always suggested being stuck in a rut with no incentive to move on, whereas the new distinction and a new attitude concerning being "a new creature in Christ" provides a glorious challenge to, **[1 Peter 1: 13], "Gird up the loins of our [spiritual] minds"** and, **[Hebrews 6: 1-3], "go on unto perfection"**, to the **[Job 4: 21], "Resurrection of the Excellency" which is in you, lest ye die, even without wisdom."**

NOTES

NOTES

I. AREA OF SERVICE

[Deuteronomy 30: 19-20], "I call heaven and earth to record this day against you, that I have set before you life and death, blessing and cursing: *therefore* choose life, that both thou and thy seed may live: vs. 20, That thou mayest love the Lord thy God, and that thou mayest obey his voice, and that thou mayest cleave unto him: for he is thy life, and the length of thy days; *that thou mayest dwell in the land which the Lord sware unto thy fathers, to Abraham, to Isaac, and to Jacob, to give them*".

It is this last portion of vs. 20 that I would like to address here, but this portion of the verse refers back to the former part. We will examine this relationship in the next paragraph. There is no doubt that the people being referred to here primarily were the Israelites; but are they the only ones to whom this portion of the verse applies?

The land referred to is a geographical area, howbeit, a very important one, but are there other things that might be referred to as areas or places where people are called to for special services such as an area of teaching or special ministries such as music or in-depth teachings and training in various things regardless of their geographical location. **[Ephesians 4:11-16]**; several areas of ministry are mentioned in verse **11** with the next 5 verses giving the reasons for which they were and are given. Now we might find the last part of verse 11 reading something like this, as pertaining to you and I, **[Acts 17:28]**, *"that thou mayest live and move and have your being in Christ, dwelling in the area of service wherein the Lord thy God has called and placed you for his glory and your profit".*

This area of service may well be any number of things God has in mind in your particular situation, **[Ephesians 4: 11-12], "And he gave some, apostles; and some, prophets; and some, evangelists; and some, pastors and teachers; For the perfecting of the saints for the work of the ministry, for the edifying of the body of Christ"**. Allow Him to do the picking, placing, and conditioning, and your life will be filled with his blessings. Get out of step with God and you will have insurmountable problems until you come back into line with his will, design, and purpose for your life. This is true of individuals, nations, and everything in between.

Now let's go back and examine these verses, **[Deuteronomy 30: 19-20]**, a little closer, performing some **"Bible Biology"**, by dissecting them in order to give them a closer examination and extracting some revelation and vital inspiration from them that is essential to our Biblical character development and maturity. In doing this we will bring in other scriptures to give us greater insight into what it is trying to teach us. In the first portion we find God providing availability of life and blessing for the people and the method and direction for obtaining this life and blessing. This "obtaining" of life and blessing is based on simply making an *intelligent, correct choice* which God himself commands us to make.

We can find New Testament input on this in **[John 3: 16]**, where God provided "life and blessing" in the person of Our Lord and Saviour, Jesus Christ, and the same method and direction for obtaining this provision, **"intelligent choice"**. There are instances when this choice is made out of desperation to get out of a very destructive life style that is akin to "death and cursing". Nevertheless, the correct choice being made, even prompted by desperation, will, if done in sincerity with the appropriate follow through of obedience, produce great and glorious benefits, both temporal and eternal. Nothing magical happens just because you made the correct choice in securing your salvation through Jesus. However, placing yourself under God's care and jurisdiction, you will begin to realize some changes taking place. Life finally begins to have meaning and purpose. **[Hebrews 6: 9]** speaks of **"better things that accompany salvation"**. These are the things that make salvation productive in your life to the bearing of **"good fruit"** and it all starts with obedience, studying the word to find out what you are to be obedient to, and examining the principles of God's truth and absolutes that translate into life and life more abundantly.

In our verse in **Deuteronomy,** God has instructed the people to choose life in which the blessing is contained. In **[John 3: 16],** the same idea is expressed by "whosoever *believeth* in him", or once again, *chooses life,* will receive the **"blessing of life and life more abundantly"**, **[John 10: 10]**. That admonition is more directly addressed in **[Matthew 17: 5]**, as God spoke out of a cloud, saying; **"This is my beloved Son, in whom I am well pleased;** *HEAR YE HIM"*. Once again we have words in which are contained the same meaning. First is the command to *"therefore choose life"*, next is the admonition to choose to *"believe in him"* for the purpose of obtaining "everlasting life". Third is a declaration from God concerning the relationship between the Father and the Son, followed immediately with the command" *hear ye Him"*. The last two are both contained in the first one with the command to **"therefore choose life"** with a compelling reason for doing so, **"so that both thou and thy seed may live"**.

Any two of the three would be contained within the third one. **Choose life; believe in him; hear ye him,** all have the unspoken concept of **"OBEDIENCE"** woven into them. This concept of "obedience" is found throughout the Old and New Testaments. Preceding, and included in obedience, is the command to **"Repent and believe the gospel, [Mark 1: 15].** With the above in mind, our scripture now reads **"Repent and believe the gospel unto obedience"**. This comprises the **"beginning of wisdom"** as is taught in **[Psalms 111: 10; Proverbs 9:10],** and alluded to in many other scriptures. This should give the reader a general idea and introduction into the art of "Biblical Biology", by using scripture to "add to" the meaning of other scripture to give greater impact to the truths contained in each, thus contributing to, and enriching our knowledge of the whole.

Now we go to **verse 20**, of **[Deuteronomy 30]**, from which this whole idea of **"Area of Service"** came with some additional insight from the **Book of Joshua** *with the arrangement of the Israelites in their travels and settlements.* It is through this experiential process of *choosing Life, believing Him, hearing Him,* and **"living and moving and having our being in Him, dwelling where and how God desires, [Acts 17: 20], that we learn to "love the Lord thy God, obey His voice, cleave unto Him, and prosper in this relationship"**. Repentance for instance, is not a one shot thing that is done at the beginning of your relationship with the Lord to initiate that relationship, and then forgotten, but is an ongoing necessity that is spoken of in **[Mark: 1-4; Luke 3:3; Acts 13:24 and 19: 4], as a "baptism of repentance"**. Considering our propensity to sin and displease God even though we are saved, this is a necessary attitude to build, sustain and enrich our individual relationship with our Lord, being grateful for God's abundance of amazing grace.

If we do not have a sense of sorrow for the things we do that displease God, we need to go back and examine our problem that is injurious to this relationship. Rest assured; if there is any correcting to be done, it will be on your side of the issue. As we learn to correct these problems, we are learning to **"love the**

Lord thy God, obey his voice, and cleave unto Him, realizing more as we grow in the grace and knowledge of the Lord, that He is indeed our life and the length of our days".**

It is through this process we also learn to live in the **"Area of Service"** wherein he has chosen to place us, whether or not it is in a specific geographical location. **[Ephesians 4:11], "And he gave some apostles; and some prophets; and some evangelists; and some pastors and teachers; for the perfecting of the saints, for the work of the ministry, for the edifying of the body of Christ".**

Who knows, he might even call some of us to be writers. In the greatness of His unlimited abilities He is not restricted to the small list found in the scripture above. We need to release him from the smallness of our finite mentalities and allow Him to be who, and what He is, and just learn to walk with him in **"the new and living way", [Hebrews 10: 20],** he has provided through Jesus Christ our Lord and Saviour. **[Proverbs 3: 5-6], "Trust in the Lord with all thy heart; and lean not unto thine own understanding. In all thy ways acknowledge him, and** *he will direct thy paths".*

Regardless of the geographical area God places you or where you find yourself for whatever reason, obedience in service unto the Lord is required in that area, capacity, or place we find ourselves. The areas of service are unlimited. I have heard it said that we are only limited by our imagination, but Biblical gained wisdom, knowledge, and understanding will certainly expand and enrich the horizons of our mental capabilities and have a profound effect on our imaginations. Meditations are an essential part of a Biblical orientated thinking mind to feed productive, scriptural imaginations based on truth and conditioned on the input of **[John 14:26].**

In **[Psalms 1: 1-3]**, The man mentioned in verse 1 doesn't do the things mentioned there because he is preoccupied with obedience to verse 2, **"But his *delight* is in the law, WORD, of the Lord; and in his WORD doth he MEDITATE day and night"**. *He lives and moves and has his being; everything subjected to, contained in, and performed within the direction, correction, counsel, and guidance, of God's Word. God's counsel and direction become his lifestyle.* Adopting the attitude and example of Jesus in **[John 4: 34]**, **"his meat, sustenance, purpose, strength, desire, etc, was to do the will of the Father, who called and commissioned him"**. God's counsel, will, and direction was his lifestyle.

A job becomes an area of ministry when it is performed with a Biblical orientated attitude. Whatever we do, tempered with Godly wisdom, becomes a ministry when our attitude toward it is under the direction of Biblical counsel and guidance. **[1Corinthians 10: 31], "Whether ye therefore eat, or drink, or whatsoever ye do, *do all to the glory of God*"**.

We find here another blending together of scriptures as we consider **[Matthew 6:33]** in conjunction with **[Psalms 1: 1-3]**. **"Seeking first the kingdom of God and his righteousness"** would certainly coincide with **"Delighting in God's Word and meditating in it day and night"**. So here are two different formations of words, both culminating in the same thing, the establishing of a lifestyle wherein the presence of God is experienced continually. These two portions of scripture fit in perfectly with **[John 8: 29]** where Jesus tells us that **"He who sent me is with me"** the Father hath not left me alone; *because* **I do always those things that please Him"**. **Diligently seeking first the kingdom of God and His righteousness, delighting in and meditating in the Word of God day and night, and living and moving and having our being in Him are all commensurate with "doing always** those things that please God". There are many other things of course that can be included here, but this is a good start to spark your own thoughts and study, expanding the horizons of your own Bible orientated mentality and imaginations.

Now let's proceed to analyze the benefits and rewards that are a result of **"doing always those things that please God"**. As a suggestion at this point, allow me to call your attention to **[Hebrews 11: 6]** for your examination and consideration for including it in with the scriptures we have studied. It fits nicely in with them with **its introduction of faith for the pleasure of God, believing that He is, and that he is a *rewarder* of them that diligently seek him, his kingdom and his righteousness.**

None of these rewards are listed here, so let's go back to some previous scriptures to get an idea of what some of them might be. Neither does **[Matthew 6: 33]** give any lists, but simply tells us that **"all these things that the Father knows you have need of, verse 32, will be added unto you"**. **[Psalms 1: 3]** gives us a good, over all idea of the content of all these benefits and rewards for these who abstain from **the counsel of the ungodly"** but fulfill the requirements of the scriptures mentioned previously.

Here is a description of this person who is faithful in his **"Area of Service"**, *geographical, physical, and spiritual,* **Verse 3, "And he shall be like a tree planted by the rivers of water, that bringeth forth his fruit in his season; his leaf also shall not wither;** *and whatsoever he doeth shall prosper"*. There is so much in this scripture that is contained in other scriptures that it amazes me, but then again that's God. He is utterly amazing.

When I first took real notice of verse 3, I thought to myself, I would sure like to be like that person that it speaks of. And from the master teacher of the universe who teaches us all things and bring all things to our remembrance came the impression, *you can be, just DO what it says in verse 2, delight in, meditate on, love [Psalms 119:165, study [2 Timothy 2: 15], and be a doer of my Word [James 1: 25], abiding therein. [2 Peter 1:4], "Whereby are given unto us exceeding great and precious promises: that by these ye might be partakers of the divine nature, having escaped the corruption that is in the world through lust"*. What a beautiful win, win situation, if we will just DO IT.

Spousal relationships become extremely important ministries with their accompanying rewards and blessings when accomplished according to Bible principles and directions. These same spousal relationships become in many cases trials of endurance or total disasters when they are not Biblically based and grounded. Either way; **"whatever radiates out from the marriage is going to fallout on the children bringing either life and blessing or death and cursing", [Deuteronomy 30:19].** This is an example of my theory of "radiation fallout" that affects all those who are within our sphere of influence, whether it is for good or evil. Any way you look at it, we are responsible for what we "radiate", our influence.

The standards and values have been set in place for such a union. It is up to the individuals involved to determine whether or not they will participate, **[Deuteronomy 28:47], "serving the Lord thy God with joyfulness and with gladness of heart for the abundance of all things"**. The scripture's previous to this one, **15-46,** reveals the results and curses on a people who failed to do this. This speaks of the need for service with a right attitude, an attitude of joyfulness and gladness, **verses 1-14.**

In **[Acts 2:41** we see this attitude mentioned again in reference to God's Word: in *"GLADLY* **receiving His word"**. And again in **[MARK I: 15]**, **"repenting, believing the gospel unto obedience and being baptized"**. This willing attitude of service**[Matthew 23: 11; Mark 9: 35; Luke 9: 48]** is essential wherever we are, in whatever area of service God has placed us; whether or not we are able to follow through on our willingness, being exceedingly thankful for God's amazing grace that sustains us through the "dry" times.

If we are not, at times able to physically follow through, let a willing attitude provide inspiration, encouragement, and incentive for those who are able. **[Proverbs 25:11]**, **"A word fitly spoken is like apples of gold in pictures of silver. As an earring of gold, and an ornament of fine gold;** *so is a wise reprover upon an obedient ear"*. Let us determine that when it comes our turn, it will come, sometimes frequently, that we will have **"obedient ears"**.

It may be that at any particular time, verbal encouragement is all you are able to provide along with your prayers. If so, then be encouraging, counseling with wisdom from a heart that has been conditioned and supplied with an abundance of Bible knowledge and understanding, **[Luke 6:45]** speaking life and healing rather than "biting and devouring", **[Galatians 5:15]**. We must condition ourselves in God's Word to **"add to"** and **"multiply"** God's blessing to others. This is much needed *positive* **"radiation fallout"** that is well pleasing to the Lord.

This "biting and devouring" is a natural aggressive function of the sinful nature we were all born with, **[Ephesians 2: 1-3]**. **But God,** verses **4-10,** because of his love, **[John 3: 16]**, provided a method of deliverance for us through Jesus Christ our Lord and Saviour to be set free from this death dealing nature unto a new, **"divine nature"**, **[2 Peter 1:4]** if we are so inclined and intelligent enough, or desperate enough, intelligence is the best option, to take advantage of it.

Even as Christians we have to exhibit enough intelligence to seek, study, learn, and practice **"the things that accompany salvation, "[Hebrews 6: 9]**, developing from **"babes in Christ, desiring and drinking the sincere milk of the word unto maturity, able to handle the beef steak and roast beef of the word, [Hebrews 5: 12-14; 1 Peter 2: 1-2].**

These **"things that accompany salvation"** are also "things of **[John 8:29]** that Jesus spoke of concerning his relationship and love for his Father. He gives us this as an example for our own progression of conduct, **"And he that sent me is always with me; the Father hath not left me alone; for [or because] I *do always those things that please him"*.** If you are interested and concerned about pleasing God and enjoying his continual presence, here is some instruction that even the simplest among us can understand. However this simple truth confounds even the wise of this world.

[Proverbs 1: 7],"The fear of the Lord is the *beginning* of knowledge: there is a continuation of the gaining of this knowledge, **but fools despise wisdom and instruction".**

[2 Peter 1: 4], "Whereby are given unto us exceeding great and precious promises: that by these ye might be partakers of the [His] divine nature, having escaped the corruption that is in the world through lust", [Romans 6: 17-19], "But God be thanked, that ye *were* [past tense] the servants of sin, but now ye have obeyed [from the heart] that form of doctrine that was delivered you. Being made free from [the bondage of] sin, ye became servants of righteousness. I speak after the manner of men because of the infirmity of the flesh: for as ye have [past tense] yielded

your members servants to uncleanness and to iniquity unto iniquity; *even so now* [present and future tense] *yield your members servants to righteousness unto holiness, doing always those things that please the Lord".*

The message is; with at least the same intensity you served sin, now serve **righteous and holiness,** increasing your intensity as you gain wisdom, knowledge and understanding. This would be the height of intelligence. The challenge is immense, but the present and eternal rewards and benefits for this obedience are beyond our comprehension. Be assured, it will cost you nothing to accept this challenge and live it to the uttermost *in comparison to what it will cost you to turn your back on it and walk away in rejection of it.*

Being in service to God and operating within his calling on your life go together like wisdom and intelligence blending together in unity of purpose; that purpose being to bring glory and honour to God, **doing always those things that please Him, [John 8:29].** Service to God and man will always be within the calling He has placed on your life regardless of where or what it is.

These callings will change from time to time which will necessitate a change in your conduct of service, not your attitude and behavior. Your behavior and service will always be the same, however the calling of a wife or husband will be different than it was in the courting stage of life. The requirement of conducting oneself honorably in relationship to the other still remains the same, but the duties and responsibilities expand and intensify as the relationship is enriched and becomes more intense, meaningful, and beautiful.

Most young people getting married haven't had the experience of being spouses as yet and will have to learn this as they go through the growing pains of emotions and feelings of being a spouse with the new responsibilities, duties, and obligations along with the privileges, which also need to be handled honorably. Hopefully they will have qualified parents and knowledgeable friends who are willing and able to assist and guide them through the inevitable difficult times and rejoice with them in the good times.

It is hoped that they will be wise enough to listen and learn, having the essential "obedient ears". Thus the difficult times become less difficult as they realize that help and loving care is close at hand. This does not release them from learning and exercising Godly wisdom, understanding, and knowledge, which takes time to accumulate, oftentimes through trial and error, but best learned through competent counseling and listening to good advice from the elders, providing the elders are competent for counsel and good advice. Not all of them are. Use discretion in selection of any needed counselors.

Now comes a child into this relationship and the behavior and service unto the Lord remain the same, but the calling of husband and wife suddenly expand to that of father and mother. Now we have additional and new responsibilities to incorporate into our time frame of 24 hours in a day without allowing our old duties and responsibilities to go by the wayside. Room and time must be made for this new responsibility in the lives of both father and mother, which if approached and handled properly with correct attitudes will enrich their lives together considerably.

Dad's responsibilities as provider enlarge and intensify as does Mom's as homemaker and caretaker. Dad's duties and responsibilities as provider includes, but extends way beyond the financial considerations to leader, teacher, trainer, conditioner of this, or these, as time goes by, young minds and lives. He must do this as he remains deeply considerate of this wife who consented to entrust not only her own life, but the lives of their children to this husband who, probably unknowingly, took on these responsibilities when he asked this beautiful young lady to become his wife and the mother of their children, possibly being a bit mesmerized at the time of the proposal. All of a sudden the "areas of service" have enlarged and intensified. New responsibilities have presented themselves to us and must be attended to "decently and in order" to produce the increased joy and peace that will accompany them, if, of course done as per God's counsel and directions, "decently and in order".

Mom on the other hand, consented to take on the responsibilities that God has outlined for a wife and mother when she accepted this proposal of marriage. There are scriptures concerning the wife as a partner in material provision for the family in **[Proverbs 31:10-31].** This is all part of the plan of God for his people as the mother teaches and sets the example for her daughters in the arts of being a wife and mother in her relationship to her husband, home, and family. Every bit and at least equally so, must dad teach, train, and set the Biblical examples for his sons. Unfortunately our world and nation are suffering a horrible breakdown in these areas.

Over the years we have heard how that a wife is to be submissive to her husband. This is by Biblical directive and as such there is no argument with that: but let's get it in proper perspective, starting with the beginning. **[Ephesians 5:25]**, **"Husbands, love your wives, even as Christ loved the church, and gave himself for it".** What does it mean to love?

As God has commanded husbands to love their wives as he loves the church, is this not a calling of service and conduct of obedience unto himself wherein he can now bless us in this relationship because of our obedience? If we as Christians can enjoy a relationship of submission to God because of his love and care of us, would not this make it desirable for a wife to be submissive to a husband who established a Christ-like relationship of love, provision, and nurturing with her? As God's king and priest in the home and before Him, the husband's privilege's, responsibilities, and duties, are many. But as rewarding and glorious as they are, they are equally as necessary and significant to the safety and harmony of the home as he dedicates "gives" himself to the care and nurturing of his wife while guiding the raising of the children as Christ has nurtured the church and given us Biblical principles of righteousness for guidance and development unto maturity.

This is not dependent on being in a geographical location. Even in the land of promise of the Israelites, this relationship of love and obedience to God is required as it is in all the rest of the world. The requirement is universal, **"Ye must be born again"**. The command is universal, **[Mark 1:15], "Repent and believe the gospel",** believing it unto willing, joyful obedience for the glory, honour, praise, and pleasure of God **"for the abundance of all things"**, **[Deuteronomy 28:47].**

Our geographical area is not our concern, although some areas are definitely more desirable than others, but, our area of calling and service to the Lord are to be taken seriously wherever we may be, and the only place we will be content is where he chooses to place us. Generally speaking, it doesn't make any difference where we are as long as we are in diligent service to Him, but specifically speaking, if there is a special place he wants you for a particular purpose, he knows how to get you there.

However, where you are now is of the primary concern at the present time. Having God's call on your life for service must be considered in your present state of being. If you think that being a missionary to be the utmost calling, then consider serving as a missionary where you are presently at, in your family, in your community, at your profession, or job, or wherever. The definition of a missionary is not so cut and dried that you have to do something that conforms to traditional definitions and customs. It basically boils down to a person who is undertaking a mission of proclaiming the gospel of Jesus Christ. If this doesn't show and is pursued in your lifestyle today, it won't do much good to talk about doing it tomorrow.

There is a great deal of emphasis put on the Israelites being in, and being in control of the land that God promised them through Abraham, Isaac, and Jacob. This will happen regardless of the opposition against God and his agenda for the Jewish nation.

But regardless of this taking place, obedience to God's Word will determine the individuals relationship with God, whether or not that individual is a Jew or whether or not that person is in a certain geographical location. The universal requirement still remains unchanged; **"Repent ye and believe the gospel"**, **[Mark 1: 15]**, and **"Ye must be born again"**, **[John 3: 7]**. **[2 Peter 3:9], "The Lord is not slack concerning his promise, as some men count slackness; but is longsuffering toward us-ward, not willing that any should perish,** *but that all should come to repentance"*.

In case some still wonder what God's will is; *it is that all should come to repentance.* This must be done as a prerequisite to all that is to follow. Whatever we can do to facilitate this is well pleasing to the Lord, establishing: **[Proverbs 11:30], "The fruit of the righteous is a tree of life;** *and he that winneth souls is wise"*. The wise become a tree of life, producing the righteous fruit of eternal life for men by winning them to our Lord and Saviour Jesus Christ, **"in whom dwelleth all the fullness of the Godhead bodily"**, **[Colossians 2: 9].**

The idea of being called of God to be a tree of life, producing fruit of righteousness is a rather intriguing thought worthy of further study and exploration. This is an area all the redeemed are called to live in, **[Acts 17:28], "For in Him we live and move and have our being"; in Him we have our function and reason for being; in Him we find purpose and fulfillment; the peace that passes understanding with fullness of joy unspeakable and full of glory, [Philippians 4:7; 1 Peter 1:8].**

There are many scriptures that lend credibility to this concept, it's possibility and, if we can get our spiritual ducks in line, its probability and finality. For unto this are we called, **to be about our Father's business, [Luke 2:49]: in the Area of Service** where He chooses to place us. **[Ephesians 2:10], "For we are his workmanship, created in Christ Jesus unto good works,** *which God hath before ordained that we should walk in them".* I have no argument with the **"saved by grace"** doctrine, for indeed we are. There is another concept, however, that needs to be equally declared unto all Christendom; that is **"we live and please God by willing, loving, obedience".**

The wonderful provision of "grace" was never given nor intended to replace obedience to his Word. This, pleasing Him who sent us and called us to service, is the Father's Business that we are to be about that Jesus showed himself to us as a living example. Wherever we are, this is our calling; this is our **"Area of Service"** wherever God has chosen to place us as individuals. And as individuals, there must be unity and harmony among us if we are to rise and remain above a survivalistic existence, living as God has ordained we should:

this is a prayer of Jesus our Lord, **[John 17]:** study this and blend your life into it.

NOTES

II. COMING OUT

The "Separation of Church and State" concept has created some real dilemmas, not only for the state but also for the only source of strength and help that is available as the once for all forever solution to mans problems, the "Christian Religion". The source of this S. C. S. idea is well known to all who are concerned about it and its adverse effects it has had on America in the hands and under the authority of questionable authorities, politicians, judges, etc., and the backing and support of anti-God, anti-Christian, anti-Bible individuals and groups such as the A.C.L.U., People for the American Way, etc. It is erroneous in theory, becomes necessary in practice due to certain prevailing circumstances, but never with any intelligent explanations concerning these various situations. It does make one wonder what Thomas Jefferson really had in mind when he included that phrase in his letter to the Danbury Baptists. I am certain he did not have in mind the erroneous way it is being presented and executed today in the separation of God and people.

Obviously the People for the American Way have never gotten a proper concept of the American Way to begin with or they would have known that the American Way was based on, and anchored in, Biblical Principles from the very beginning and conception of this new nation. Apparently these people are more concerned about their own "un-American, anti-God, if it feels good, do it, self-centered, special interest, ways, than they are about the well being of America and her people. These Biblical principles were to be the foundational strength and guidance of this America as she progressed from conception, birth, infancy, and on to maturity. Whether or not America will survive to accomplish God's purpose is becoming rather questionable.

Unfortunately America was hijacked in her infancy by adverse, contrary, elements, "her own countrymen" opposed to and hostile toward the Biblical foundation that was to be her strength, direction, and purpose; and consequently maturity has never been attained to. At the present time, America is similar to a disobedient, rebellious idiot, warring against a loving parent. This maturity will take place sometime in the future, if you will pardon the expression though quite realistic in this case, God only knows when, under new management and not as a democracy that America holds so dear in her rejection of God. We find the beginning accounts of this in **[Isaiah 9: 6]** and the continuing accounts in the following verse **[7]**, which will be its final form and progression.

In our society today, much concern is expressed over the increase of government with increased controls rules, regulations, etc, that people see as a threat to their "rights and freedoms". This is understandable under the humanistic forms of government that reject God's counsel of Biblical instructions for successful government, however, there is an interesting statement concerning this a the beginning of **verse 7, "Of the increase of his, God's government under the Kingship of Jesus, AND PEACE, there shall be no end".** This is impossible under human government that operates in rejection of God's righteous counsel. Increase of man's government by mans wisdom only brings more confusion and chaos and eventual destruction. History has recorded ample proof of this.

This confusion and chaos is what we are witnessing and experiencing in our world today as individuals and nations, and is in total contrast to the "government under Jesus" that will take place in God's own timing. Nationally, as an individual, you may not be able to do much in the way of changes, but as an individual, on an individual basis, total change is only a choice away. **[Mark 1: 14-15], "And Jesus came saying, The time is fulfilled, and the kingdom of God is at hand, REPENT YE AND BELIEVE THE GOSPEL".**

The adversities forced on America by the anti-God, anti-Christ, anti-righteousness, incompetents has stunted America's growth and development process, and threatens her very existence, having already robbed her of much of her life; such life being found only in her Christian Religion roots. This life can only be resurrected by first resurrecting the Biblical teachings, principles, and roots, and reinstating them as, **"the law of the land"**. Man and his laws have shown themselves to be totally inadequate to govern a Christian nation and have reduced it to an uncontrollable chaotic mess with our illustrious leaders left wringing their hands over their loss of the ability to find a solution to our national dilemmas.

Our man made "constitution" has been in force for over two hundred years and its presence, whether in its original form and intent, or its new twisted perverted form, with threats now to some of its amendments, has not preserved nor benefited our nation, especially in the long run, for it has been, and is, in the hands and under the control of corrupted humanity. There was a time when the Biblically presented principles and teachings were esteemed as very valuable and absolutely essential in the forming of our nation, beginning in the lives of individuals who were to play foundational roles in that forming.

Since that time, man, in his corruption, has discovered a "better way" of science, using their twisted constitution, and imposing of the "rights" of every convenient form and evil invention that assists man in opposing and degrading the Christian Way of life. The result and effect is what we are witnessing in America today with her multiplied problems that are proving much to difficult for man to handle with his present low level and condition of mentality, conversation, and conduct. If man would open his eyes, be honest with himself in an assessment of his present individual and nationwide condition in relationship to the God he has rejected, maybe, just maybe, he could come up with enough intelligence to realize he needs to make some changes, such intelligence and changes to be found only in God's counsel. If he doesn't, he is going to experience a relationship of judgment that God is going to have with him he isn't going to enjoy.

Whether or not man can and will come up with enough intelligence to make the correct changes and have the courage to impose them in the face of the unquestionable opposition that would arise against such changes is another question. So far he has not shown the intelligence, inclination, or propensity to do so.

Neither has he shown the wisdom to do so; for that wisdom only has its beginning in the "fear, or revering, of God, with its continual growth and development in the continuing of reverencing and obedience to him, **[Psalms 111: 10; Proverbs 1: 7]**.

The wheel that squeaks gets the grease, and the only wheel that has shown the courage, which is in their case, is arrogance disguised as courage, to squeak, have been the wheels that are contrary to the teachings of righteousness, holiness, Godliness, purity, etc, that come from the confines of God's Word.

The sexual perverts, excuse the "political incorrectness" of the term; I do not apologize for the truth regardless of the attempts to suppress it, have come out of their closets along with every other adverse influence, squeaked and demanded their rights and have gotten the grease from the high courts while simultaneously been instrumental in pushing all that opposes them, the Christian "Religion", with whatever resultant decency is left in America, into "a closet". This "closet" is a "Corral of Compliance" wherein the Christians are herded by the erroneous rules and regulation's imposed by our "leaders" that are in opposition to the Bible and it righteous principles; but make room for everything that is of that opposition.

Certainly those with the truth of God's word should be able to exhibit enough true courage to at least hold their ground in the face of all opposition without caring about accusations of being intolerant bigots. However, this does not seem to be the case.

Who cares what those that are intolerant bigots against Christianity whine about? Let them defend their pointless position against God's truth if they can. It seems that we were already in our own closet for some time prior to this, as adverse changes began to be asserted by individuals and groups, that themselves, in opposition to the gospel of God, were taking control of the American stage. Being intolerant and bigoted against the teachings of the gospel, made them acceptable to the general public at large with their anti-Bible practices that catered to the "if it feel good, do it" sinful nature of man. They began crowding out, displacing, and replacing what had been up to that time, Americas Christian principles, teaching, and practices. While all this was happening and the Christian community went on a passive defense so as not to offend anyone, they affectively abdicated their position and authority. Enter now, The Separation of Church and State, with its opposition to the establishment and promotion of these "Christian principles, teachings, and practices" that God had given us *as the life's blood of our nation.*

Enter now, the "politically correct" embracing of every contrary religion, philosophy, concept, or whatever man desires that opposes the Christian Experience of truth and absolutes; this embracing all being done in the name of political correctness, tolerance, relativity, and diversity, etc. Now I will have to refrain from using the word "religion" in conjunction with "Christian" unless they are used together to identify the specific religion: "Christian" being referred to. Due to the advent of multiplied adverse, contrary, religions, the use of the term "religion" has been forced to take on the quality of just being generic and lumping Christianity in with the rest of the religions. From a Christian's viewpoint, this is inexcusable, intolerable, and totally unacceptable; this view itself being "politically incorrect" and offensive to the enemies of the cross of Jesus".

Our governing "authorities" don't seem to have the intelligence to recognize the nationally destructive nature of this "legally enforced" ungodly union which has favored these contrary religions and sinful practices. This should not be construed in such a way to imply that I have no respect of these contrary religions; I claim to have the same respect for them as God himself has; as soon as you can determine the level of respect that God has for them and the promoters of them, you will understand my position on them. Surly you cannot expect a Christian to feel any different about them than God himself feels about them. I doubt very much that God is concerned about complying with political correctness either. If this is politically incorrect and offends the political correct mob, so be it. **Biblical correctness trumps political correctness any time, all the time, and every time, and everywhere.** I don't care who disagrees with me, including the government, the supreme courts, lower courts, or the ACLU, and even some professing Christian brethren, **"mine own countrymen", [2 Corinthians 11: 26].**

If the Bible is not the priority in the Christians life, I would have to question if that persons experience extends beyond a mere profession, as it must, if there is to be a genuine relationship with God. **You can belong to a religion or even be religious without repentance, but you cannot have a born again, cleansed by the blood of Jesus, intimacy of relationship with God without repentance. Ye must be born again.**

What we, as Christians have, is what God established and intended from the beginning, that all men everywhere should have a close personal relationship with him yesterday, today and forever. Regardless of what man believes that is contrary to this Biblical teaching and revelation; man without God is nothing, has nothing, and can become nothing but an ever increasing irritant to God, himself, and his fellow man, which is an extremely foolish position to choose to be in. Nevertheless, this does seem to be the rut wherein humanity has chosen to wallow.

Thank God for the exceptions that have exercised enough intelligence to choose the **"new and living way" [Hebrews 10: 19-24], the "strait gate and narrow way that leads to life everlasting, [Matthew 7: 13-14; Luke 13: 24]** that God has lovingly provided through Jesus Christ. Whether or not man makes his choice based on intelligence in response to "the goodness of God that leadeth men to repentance" or simply out of a desperate attempt to escape the idiocy of this world, makes no difference; God is able to meet the need of the lost desperate soul, bring peace to the troubled heart and healing to the confused, wayward mind.

God provided the church, through Jesus Christ, as the avenue, the conduit, for his message of salvation and deliverance from a sin sick, lost, dying, and condemned world.

Unfortunately, human governments have been notorious in their reputations for blocking these means of communications of God's message with a variety of methods, many of which were and continue to be violent and deadly. Others have been a bit more discreet in their methods, but the object of opposing and stopping the flow of God's word remains the same. Such is the erroneous ungodly concept of the so-called constitutional "Separation of Church and State".

I use the word "ungodly" here as this whole idea seems to be aimed at the Christian Religion, church, faith, experience, or whatever term is used to identify the establishment of Christianity. Regardless of the faults and failings of the "Christian" church, it is still God's conduit of Biblical transmission to a lost and dying world. If a government or other "pseudo" authority under or within that governmental structure is allowed to plug this "conduit" by rules, regulations, laws, or whatever, they are responsible for the "Separation of God and People".

Civil authorities have attempted to shift all responsibility for religious input from themselves, to the people, to the "churches", *thus hoping to relieve themselves of any obligations or responsibilities* to, and for the spiritual training and eternal salvation of their charges or subjects. Thus do they contribute heavily to the destruction of themselves, their families, societies, and the nations for which they are responsible and have sworn to serve, guide, and protect. In the promotion of their Christian duties and obligations of the Christian hierarchy; the church, with its Biblical principles as the foundational strength of that nation, should be able to depend on and enjoy the protection of the civil government as overseers and protectors of the entire nation: such government jealously guarding these Biblical principles for the continuing well-being and strength of this nation. Unfortunately they have been instrumental in suppressing them and destroying their promotion. We are experiencing the graphic effects of this today throughout our beloved America, **[Isaiah 5: 24; Hosea 4: 6-7],** *the "blossoms" of verse 24 being the children of verse 6.*

Any people, whether it be church, state, nation, or whatever, so denied this source of Godly counsel, ordained by Biblical input, influence, conditioning and training, is in a situation where we find blind followers forced into conditions of blindness by their blind leaders. This forced blindness is due to the devilish imposition of means "legally", by law, to interrupt and stop this flow of Biblical transmitted knowledge, **the lack of which destroys whole nations and people, [Hosea 4:6].**

We can see this process of destruction taking place in our nation today, taking a terrible toll on all ages of people beginning with the even as yet, unborn and goes or from there to include all manner of filth and degradation in all ages. None are immune to sin and its devastating effects in their own life or the lives of others, especially those close to them. Evil in its many devious methods of destruction also is no respecter of persons. We can however, through Jesus and conformity to God's word, become non-participants, thus greatly reducing the effects of self imposed transgressions and their penalty. We are still affected by the sinfulness of others, which effects we are seeing, feeling, and experiencing every day.

Love demands this and sensitivity to the pain of others, and concern for their over all well-fare will not allow us to be otherwise. Praying for them may be all we can do, but it will be the best and most we can do in the majority of cases. There are, of course, other things that we can do, depending on the situation at hand such as **[Proverbs 25:11-12], "A word fitly spoken is like apples of gold in pictures of silver. As an earring of gold, and an ornament of fine gold, so is a wise** reprover upon an obedient ear". It is important to note here that, **"an obedient ear"** is a necessary component of the equation in obtaining the desired results. Unfortunately, obedient ears, especially to Biblical truths and absolutes, are becoming increasingly scarce, not yet a rarity, but still scarce, being partial to the "few" exceptions of **[Matthew 7: 13]**, mentioned earlier, among the American population as well as the rest of the world.

[Acts 2:41]," Then they that gladly received *"with obedient ears"* **his word were baptized: and the same day there were added unto them about three thousand souls.** Obedient ears are hard to come by these days, **[Proverbs 1:7], "The fear of the Lord is the beginning of knowledge, but fools despise wisdom and instruction".** It is vitally essential that spiritually deaf ears be "born again" to ears that will hear as willing receivers of God's transmission of truth instead of wallowing in the continual deceiving, confusing static of this world.

Transmission of Biblical truths, and the necessity of embracing them unto proper attitudes of obedience, has always been better than the receiving "equipment" on the other end of the transmission. Consequently the fools of this world with their disobedient ears continue to cast God behind them, despise his word of wisdom and instruction and never acquire the knowledge that is a result of fearing "revering" God: **such knowledge as is necessary to prevent their destruction, [Hosea 4:6].**

It is an unfortunate thing that so many of the positions of authority, thus influence, are held by so many of the "fools" referred to in **[Proverbs 1:7],** just mentioned, and our whole nation is experiencing the destructive results. This was common throughout history; we have not learned from it, and so are doomed to continue to repeat it, having chosen rather, to remain an ignorant nation, and people. To learn these lessons is to gain knowledge unto life and blessing; to not learn them and learn them well enough to not repeat the errors of disobedience and rebellion, is to not gain, but reject, the knowledge needed to prevent self-destruction.

Some of this knowledge is to be gained from observing the misfortunes of others; some of it from experiencing our own misfortunes due to our own disobedience; still some of this knowledge is gained by diligently studying God's word, and applying the principles stated therein. This being the intelligent, preferred method for gaining knowledge; isn't it amazing how the masses have so vehemently rejected it and cast it away; **[Isaiah 5: 24],** thus taking the lumps of idiocy on their own heads for not learning from the lumps those who have gone before us have already taken.

This, of course, would be the way of wisdom, a Godly quality and characteristic, that man in his ignorance and rejection of God and his absolutes, has not yet acquired, even among some segments of Christendom. One need not experience a problem to learn a lesson if one is intelligent enough to observe the lumps on the other fellows head, then study to show themselves approved unto God, **[2 Timothy 2: 15]; [Acts 10:35], "reverence God and work righteousness"**, thus avoiding similar lumps, bumps and related problems.

It is amazing the amount and severity of lumps we personally seem to have to experience before a dawning begins to break in our own mentalities. Even as Christian's, there is a propensity for having very hard heads in conjunction with other attributes that continue to plague us. God, however, is very patient. As long we insist on the foolish, miserable, tolerating of these things that he has warned us away from: he will allow it. **[Hosea 5: 15]**

After taking enough painful lumps, we begin to realize there is a better way, and **[Romans 2: 4]** begins to capture our attention with it's message about riches, goodness, forbearance, longsuffering, and repentance. We begin to realize that if we want the blessings contained in this message, *maybe we should get real serious about the repentance required to obtain them.*

Somehow we are not experiencing the blessings promised when we accepted Jesus as Lord and Saviour, and doubts begin to creep in. We have been going to church and Sunday School like we were told that Christians should, but something is missing. I have been taking my Bible with me when I go to meetings, even reading the verses referred to in church and Sunday School class, but something is still missing. I have repented of my sins and turned away from them. I even read the Bible occasionally and hear it preached in church, but maybe, just maybe, this does not constitute being "a doer of the word".

Maybe there's more to this than just putting in my appearance at church every Sunday morning, hearing a sermon, a Sunday school lesson, shaking the preachers hand on the way out, exchanging a few niceties with a few people, them going home to start the process all over again. Some where in the recesses of my mind there is a scripture about **"studying to show thyself approved unto God, a workman that needeth not to be ashamed, rightly dividing the word of truth", [2 Timothy 2: 15].** This is when and where the realization of the essentials of obedience begin to set in and make sense.

Then it dawns on me. Repenting of sin and turning away from them is necessary, but in turning away from them, I need *to turn to something* to fill the void that the absence of sin left.

Ah yes; the **"delighting in the word, meditating on it day and night, studying it, loving it, doing it: all these things to create a new good, God pleasing abundance of the heart to produce good fruit and a renewing of the mind;** that has to be the answer, *the things that accompany salvation that please God.* Just for exercise, match these scriptures to the highlighted portion of this paragraph, **[Psalms 1: 2; 2 Timothy 2: 15; Psalms 119: 165; James 1: 22; Luke 6: 45; Matthew 7: 17; Romans 12: 2, Hebrews 6: 9; John 8: 29].** Isn't it amazing how all this boils down to one thing, **"obedience"**! Only man could make something this simple so ridiculously complicated.

Maybe a program of intense study of God's word is in order to find the "things" that are missing that somehow I know are there somewhere, if I can just find them. I wonder if an intense, diligent study of God's word would assist and enable me to learn how to use this "sword of the Spirit" with proficiency, and to keep this proficiency sharp for effective application. I perceive great value in this and know that there is a definite connection here if I can just get it sorted out and get it put together and organized in my mind.

This scripture **in [John 14:26], "But the Comforter, which is the Holy Ghost, whom the Father will send in my name, he shall teach you all things and bring all things to your remembrance, whatsoever I have said unto you",** must have a direct bearing on what is happening in my life concerning where these thoughts are coming from and who is responsible for their revelation to me, as to the remembrance of them. Maybe studying to be a "doer of the word, not just a hearer", or disinterested reader, compelled by tradition and custom would have a bearing on what seems to be missing.

Maybe studying to find out and applying these **"things" in [Hebrews 6:9] that accompany the salvation of the soul is** necessary for the enrichment of this salvation experience. However, if I learn them, I will have to study them to blend my life with them so they become characteristic of my life. What a glorious challenge to be sure. This must have some bearing on what **[John 8: 29]** is referring to where Jesus speaks of the **"Father as never leaving him alone for I do always those things that please him"**. Always enjoying the presence of the Father by **"doing always those things that please him"**: what a wonderful concept and beautiful revelation.

It sounds amazingly like being obedient and **"serving the Lord with joyfulness and gladness of heart for the abundance of all things", [Deuteronomy 28: 47],** which mankind has shown a strong tendency to reject and even many as Christians to neglect. I wonder if incorporating and blending my life into the **"fruit of the Spirit",[Galatians 5: 22-23]** might just be some of the "things" considered here along with forgiveness, patience, understanding, wisdom, and a host of other things found throughout God's instruction manual for life, the Bible, would be in order.

This is going to take some time of deep meditation to sort all this out and get it in order. It makes one thankful that the Holy Spirit, the master instructor of the universe is always present, ready, willing, and certainly able with his extreme patience, to assist in our quest for knowledge, direction and clarity in the application of these "things". But we as individuals have to want to pursue these "things". As I have heard it said; *"you gotta wanna"*. **[Colossians 3: 2], "Set your affection on things above, not on things on the earth".**

You will go in the direction you wanna go, whether it be right or wrong, good or evil. Your level and condition of intelligence will determine this, barring any exterior obstacles or obstructions. *From the abundance of the heart the mind thinketh, the mouth speaketh, and the hand doeth. We are all victimized or set free by our mentalities.* **[Proverbs 23: 7], "As a man thinketh in his heart, mind, so is he".**

If a man's heart is truthful, his words are truth, if his heart is evil, he may speak the same words, but they will be spoken with deception of mind. **[Proverbs 4:23], "Keep thy heart with all diligence; for out of it are the issues of life".** The implication here is that the heart, mind, soul, and spirit of a man, his total being, is to be diligently kept, nurtured, supplied, and conditioned, from the abundance of God's Word and counsel. Thus this man, women, whoever, becomes a source of strength, encouragement, and help, adding much to the lives of those around them, becoming a **"tree of life, bearing the good fruit of righteousness", [Proverbs 11: 30].** This is good "radiation fallout" pleasing to, and blessed of the Lord.

This whole process and state of being becomes a condition of prosperity of the soul, **[3 John: 2], "Beloved, I wish above all things that thou mayest prosper and be in health, even as thy soul prospereth".** This all is contingent on the total person being DILIGENTLY kept, taught, and influenced from within the boundaries and confines of God's Word. Those whose priorities are not in the Bible will have a tendency to let their "diligence" go by the wayside and turn aside, little by little, very subtly, unto things that bring poverty to the soul rather than maintaining and pursuing additional soul prosperity. These hearts, not being "diligently kept and minds not being renewed" issue and produce death rather than life. Do not victimize yourself with a spiritually defective, non-Bible influenced and conditioned, mentality; such a mentality that defiles, works abomination, and is deceptive, deceiving yourself, **[James 1: 22], "But be ye doers of the word, and not hearers only, deceiving your own selves".**

[Revelation 21:27, " And there shall in no wise enter in to it [God's New Jerusalem], any thing that defileth, neither whatsoever worketh abomination, or maketh a lie: but they which are written in the Lamb's book of life", "those who have kept their heart with all diligence, those whose priority is to do always those things that please him"]. These three things; *that which defileth, worketh abominations and maketh lies,* are the very things that are insidiously and subtly forcing themselves on our American society and today, making policy, and characterizing our culture.

These things are protected by the imposition of a twisted constitution that has been described as the "law of the land". Man is responsible for this. Whenever this happens in any society, those who are responsible for the twisting and perversion of the law, by their deception, become the rulers and dictators of the land: even though they are evil and serving in a democracy. *The Word of God is rejected, despised, and cast away with its life giving wisdom, understanding, knowledge, and God's counsel*, **thus the people are destroyed, [Hosea 4:6].**

It may take a while, but we can see this foolishness in its deceptive, destructive progress all around us every day. Our society is thoroughly contaminated with it. Consequently, **[Job 4:20], "The people are destroyed from morning to evening: they perish forever without any regarding it"**. It is amazing how people are being destroyed from morning to evening and welcome it because it is a result of, and feeds their worldly orientated "if it feels good, do it" mentality.

If these people are prone to "come out" of their closets with their abominations, and degradations for polluting and spreading their filth of destruction throughout our society: it would seem that those with the truth of God's word, regardless of the opposition with their threats and attempted intimidations, should have the courage and boldness to "come out" and bring healing, well being and soul prosperity for the life of the nation and her people without being adversely affected, intimidated, and ridiculed, by those opposed to it. Mans mind takes on some strange twists in its function. The Christians have the truth that sets men and nations free from spiritual bondage, but we have been "legally" hampered in our efforts to promote it as it restricts the sinful activity of the "if it feels good, do it crowd, who comprise the "many", the bulk of humanity.

As a matter of fact, it would seem that intelligence and a desire for a better way of life would support and demand this "coming out"; the declaring and proclaiming of God's delivering truth, even if it were just viewed as a possibility, considering the death mode mankind has gotten himself locked into under the present state of his mentality and circumstances.

Maybe some Old Testament "mighty men of valor" are needed in our wayward society today. Unfortunately, we have allowed the suppression of Biblical truth in favor of the erroneously imposed human rights that have allowed all manner of ungodliness to become the norm in our American culture and society. And once again, **[Job 4: 20]** makes its appearance whether or not society likes it, or even is aware of it, or even cares.

Man cannot do away with God's absolutes simply because he chooses to reject, neglect and despise them, attempting to hide them away in his sin of unbelief. **[Romans 1: 18],"For the wrath of God is revealed from heaven against all ungodliness and unrighteousness of men, who hold,** *hide, bind, suppress, inhibit, etc,* **the truth in unrighteousness:** even though it is initiated by the state and erroneously applied to the constitution as "the separation of church and state". All he does is victimize himself by his adherence to, and promotion of the idiocy that is opposed to God's principles and absolutes.

If these people can come out of their closets of seclusion and shame, where are the Christians at in their efforts to declare and promote the gospel of Jesus Christ with all the fullness of God that is contained therein! Isn't it well nigh time for us to appear in the public forum and lift up the name of Jesus our Lord and Saviour, regardless of the opposition and what they think, or who they are? The life and success of America demands and depends on this.

By all means, God Bless America, but this is contingent on **America blessing God with love and obedience to his principles for a change.** American's, from border to border, and from sea to polluted sea, should be on their knees in thanksgiving to God for his love, mercy, grace, longsuffering, and patience, in the face of the nationwide abominations that are committed against him every day within this great nation.

I do believe, however, that His patience is wearing quite thin. Certainly if we had eyes that could see, and minds of understanding, we would see signs of his wrath beginning to seep through areas where that patience is ceasing to be. Ears to hear the crying of the starving children and hurting souls around the world that are victimized by the increasing stupidity and abominations of our world leaders who fail to encourage the promotion of the gospel of Jesus Christ would be a help in recognizing these signs of his wrath being poured out on a crooked and rebellious world, even today.

All the personal, national, international, world problems; all the confusion, chaos, calamities, tragedies, etc, etc, that we see and hear about are only symptoms of one great underlying problem of stupidity of sinful indulgences that mankind exhibits moment by moment, hour by hour, day by day, year in and year out. This is simply his willful rebellion and disobedience against God and his principles of righteousness.

In his lack of a "vision of the value" of having an intimate relationship with a loving God, man in his idiocy prefers to wallow in his abominations and filth of sin unto utter destruction and eternal torment and misery. Shakespeare only had a glimpse of the significance of this in his profound statement, **"What fools ye mortals be"**. Thus does humanity continue with their ever increasing suffering in rejection of God's out-stretched arms with hands of love and compassion even when he has provided us a solution to all our individual and collective dilemmas. **[2 Chronicles 7: 14], "If my people, which are called by my name, shall humble themselves, and pray, and seek my face, and turn from their wicked ways, THEN** [*based on the conditions just stated*] **will I hear from heaven, and will forgive their sin, and will heal their land"**.

On the heels of every national disaster, we hear the questions and insinuations that God is responsible for this and how could a loving God allow such things to happen. Isn't it amazing how this disbelieving, Godless bunch will allow themselves to consider that there just might be a God when the opportunity arises of some catastrophic event that they can blame him for in their unceasing attempts to discredit him? This, insinuating of course, that if he is real, he could not be a loving God. Isn't it amazing how this godless, disbelieving bunch will allow themselves to consider that there just might be a God when something happens they can blame him for? Allow some scripture that may cast a little light on this; that is of course, providing you are not so blinded by your pre-conditioning to see light.

[Job 5:6-7], "Although affliction cometh not forth of the dust, neither doth trouble spring out of the ground; Yet man is born unto trouble as the sparks fly upward". [Isaiah 50:11], "Behold all ye that kindle a fire; that *compass yourselves* about with sparks: walk in the light of your fire, and in the sparks *that ye have kindled.* **THIS YE SHALL HAVE OF MINE HAND;** ye shall lie down in sorrow". [Deuteronomy 30:19], "I call heaven and earth to record this day against you, that I have set before you life and death, blessing and cursing: *therefore choose life that both thou and thy seed may live".* If you choose an existence of sin with its resultant death, and cursing, **walking in the fire and among the sparks ye have kindled unto your own destruction:** rather than choosing a life of serving the Lord thy God with joyfulness and gladness of heart for the abundance of all things, his multiplied blessings: you have no one to blame but yourself for your troubles, **"therefore choose life that both thou and thy seed, descendents, may live".**

Our national, state, and local leaders in all their capacities of politicians, presidents, judges, or whatever, at all levels and everywhere must step up to the plate, repent, believe the gospel of Jesus Christ unto obedience and, **[Isaiah 64: 9], stir up themselves to take hold of God,** lead and encourage the nation to do the same, or suffer the consequences along with the nation they have neglected in their responsibilities before God.

Man may come up with idiotic excuses and lame-brained reasons to excuse themselves from such responsibilities, but God will not be put off with such non-sense. God has established government to look to the well being of the people, and the promotion of his values and principles for the good of all, not set up their own political gangs to use the people to fund and further their own self interest agendas, build their personal empires, and design laws that compel the people to not only allow such practices, but force them to support it all. Yea verily, **"What fools ye mortals be"**!

The book of **Proverbs** gives many scriptures that pertain to governments: **28: 2, 4, 5, 12, 28; 29: 2, 4.** There are many others throughout God's Word that makes an interesting and revealing study. Some ancient governments, very few, under obedient kings prospered along with their people, while others under the thumb of rebellious, sinful slobs posing as kings that were given to debauchery, **"caused all Israel to sin"**, and brought God's judgment on the entire nation.

It may be Old Testament, it may be law, call it what you will, but, it is above all, Biblical truth and principles, given originally to the Israelites, but applicable to all men everywhere. Once again read it, study it for emphasis: **[2 Chronicles 7: 14], "If my people, which are called by my name, shall humble themselves and pray, and seek my face, and turn from their wicked ways; THEN will I hear from heaven, and will forgive their sin, and will heal their land"**. "The zeal of the Lord of Hosts will perform this", **[Isaiah 9:7] and the gates of hell SHALL NOT prevail. It is COMING OUT TIME FOR THE CHURCH.**

NOTES

III. IMPOSED IMPULSES

[James 4:7],"Submit yourselves therefore to God. Resist the devil and he will flee from you". There is obviously a need here to get rid of the devil and his devices, much of what was alluded to in the previous chapter. These devices can be nothing other than his evil influences on our lives, which entrances we provide by way of our erroneous thoughts and thinking which are conditioned by what is seen, heard, felt, and otherwise experienced by way of the world we live in, the majority of which have developed a particular desire to have. **[James 4: 1],"From whence cometh wars and fightings among you: Come they not hence;** *even of the lusts that war in your members"*?

It is because of this we are commanded to, **[Romans 12:2], "Be not conformed to this world: but be ye transformed by the renewing of your mind, that ye may prove what is that good, and acceptable, and perfect will of God".** We, as a people are in desperate need of a new direction that **"Biblically renewed minds, and diligently kept hearts"** will provide for us. There are no options to this if we would prefer life and blessings over an existence of death and cursing which leads to **[Isaiah 5: 14].**

God does not give us commands to obey just because he is God, and therefore the boss who wants to be the boss, showing his authority and "throwing his weight around". This is the kind of nonsense man revels in: but God is much too great and noble to allow such smallness to exist, even in thought. He has committed himself to righteousness, to us and our eternal wellbeing. Only we intelligent human beings stand in his way and against his will. His motive for such commands is for our profit and good. Our motive for being obedient to his commands is simply because it pleases him and brings him glory and honour. The paydays are at his discretion; you can trust him to be more than fair with benefits and rewards beyond your imagination for diligent service. Disobedience to his commands leaves us out in the devil's territory where we are vulnerable to being "devoured" by this accuser and destroyer of the brethren. Using what intelligence I have; I have decided it is best to be a "non-participant" in such rebellious idiocy.

There are a multitude of scriptures that allude to and describe these situations and circumstances. We will include a number of these as we proceed in this writing. To begin, let's go to scripture that pertains directly to choices, something we all make quite often that can have a rewarding or devastating affect on our lives, *depending of course on whether our choices are correct or incorrect, right or wrong, good or evil, in accordance to God's Word, or contrary to it.* We have many in Christendom who claim that "we are not under law, but under grace" and as a result have discounted the Old Testament and its importance and thus denied themselves, and others, the tremendous wealth of wisdom, knowledge, and understanding, that is contained in it.

They somehow have misplaced, forgotten, or neglected **[2 Timothy 3: 16-17], "ALL scripture is given by inspiration of God, and is profitable for doctrine, for reproof, for correction, for instruction in righteousness: That the man of God may be perfect, thoroughly furnished unto all good works"**. With my understanding, I would have to consider "all" to include the Old Testament along with, and as a part of the New Testament for the purpose stated in the scripture. It would seem, that if the **"man of God is going to be perfect, furnished unto all good works"**, *that he would necessarily* have to do what is required to attain to such a standing of, **"being accepted with God" [Acts 10: 35].**

I have found the vast majority of Biblical principles in the Old Testament simply reinforced and emphasized in the New Testament, with due consideration given to certain aspects of the laws that were disannulled in practice but fulfilled in the person of Jesus Christ. **[Matthew 5:17], "Think not that I am come destroy the law, or the prophets: I am not come to destroy, but to fulfill".** The Old Testament established and emphasized obedience to God's word and the New Testament maintained this principle of obedience and continues to reinforce and re-emphasize it. It was not diminished simply because of the introduction and administration of God's amazing grace. Obedience is still required, though not necessarily holding a position of popularity or in vogue. **[Proverbs 29: 18], "Where there is no vision, the people perish: but he that keepeth the law, happy is he".** We need a vision of the value of obedience to God's principles, whether they are in the Old or New Testament. God's Word is still yea and amen, set in place and eternal, **[Mathew 24: 35], "Heaven and earth shall pass away, *but my words shall not pass away"*.**

Yes, we are saved by grace, but we live by obedience that flows from a willing heart and a Biblical, Holy Spirit trained and taught mind. **[Acts 17:28], "For in him we live and move and have our being", [Deuteronomy 28: 47], "Because thou servedst the Lord thy God with joyfulness and with gladness of heart, for the abundance of all things".** You will notice that I left the word "not" out of this scripture to change it from the application to disobedient and rebellious people to give it a correct meaning concerning willing servants. This word "not" will be found in verse 15 of this same chapter in reference to, once again, disobedience and rebellion. The whole of chapter 28 gives us the blessed results of obedience, those who will, verses 1-14, and the graphic results of disobedience, those who will not, verses 15-68. ***These are principles that have been set in place in the Old Testament, reinforced in the New Testament and will prevail throughout all eternity.***

"The wages of sin are still death, and the gift of God is still eternal life", [Romans 6:23]. "Jesus Christ is the same yesterday, today, and forever", [Hebrews 13:8]. His Word stands as written, revealed, and preferably taught. He has not nor will he change his mind about sin and iniquity to accommodate anyone regardless how important they think they may be, who, in their **arrogance, and ignorance have inadvertently "chosen death and cursing rather than life and blessing", [Deuteronomy 30:19]. Thus through their lack of acquired and required knowledge, have brought destruction unto themselves, their families, and entire cultures, [Hosea 4:6-7].**

External enemies have destroyed thousands, but our national internal rejection, the means of mass destruction within our minds, without the weapons; and rebellion against God and his counsel has killed it's tens of thousands unto the millions within our own borders simply because America has forgotten the word of their God and America's children are paying a horrible price for the leaders and parents transgressions. This is happening because of the sensibilities being enslaved by the "imposed impulses" that act on an "if it feels good, do it" mentality that is typical of the undisciplined minds of anti-God, anti-Bible, anti-Christ societies and cultures.

For this reason we are taught to **[Proverbs 4:23], "Keep thy heart with all diligence; for out of it are the issues of life". It follows that the un-kept heart issues forth death. [Ezekiel 18: 4, 20], "The soul that sinneth, it shall die".**

It also follows that the culture, society, and nation that condones, permits, and practices such abominations is already, in a very real sense, dead. It would seem that America, and some churches, have a lot in common with the church of Sardis in **[Revelation 3: 1-6], especially verses 1 and 2; "I know thy works that thou hast a name that thou livest, and art dead. Be watchful, and strengthen** *the things that remain, THAT ARE READY TO DIE:* in their death throes, **for I have not found thy works perfect before God"**.

[Isaiah 1:18], "Come now, and let us reason together, saith the Lord: though your sins be as scarlet, they shall be white as snow; though they be red like crimson, they shall be as wool". Reasoning together with the Lord on the basis of intellectual application and trusting in his counsel and word is the **"keeping of the heart with all diligence"**.

On this foundation of God's wisdom, knowledge, and understanding, man is able to make intelligent decisions and choices, and to remain free of the "imposed impulses" of unreliable sensibilities of the feelings and emotions, of which **[Ephesians 4:14], every wind of doctrine by the sleight of man and cunning craftiness, whereby they lie in wait to deceive,** *is comprised*, and every unreasonable and unintelligent action is founded and performed. *If wise restraint is absent in the presence of imposed impulses, trouble is sure to follow.*

This leaves us with a real problem in our post-modern society of relativity where absolutes are rejected, and as a result Biblical teachings with its truth and absolutes are scorned. What is viewed as unintelligent and unreasonable from a Christian viewpoint may be and seems to be totally acceptable in the non-Christian segment of our American society. It has even tainted some areas of the church, much to our shame.

As of the date of this writing atrocities are being reported on the news; and shown on the television daily of abominations of parents against children and children against parents and as sin and iniquity spreads among the non-Christians. Most of this is done without motives, but just on the **"imposed impulses"** of out of control sensibilities of an "if it feels good, do it culture". This has been the norm for a considerable length of time and in all likelihood will continue and increase in intensity, **[Hosea 4: 7], "As they were increased, so they sinned against me: therefore will I change their glory into shame"**. We have seen this taking place, also for a considerable length of time and we have no one to blame but ourselves for allowing our nation to digress to its present condition.

Consequently, immorality has become the norm and abortion marches on. I understand as of this date there have been approximately forty-fifty million plus, victims of the sick mentality that has perpetrated such evil. It casts a rather appalling veil of stench over the greatness of America. How terribly the mighty has fallen.

"The land of the free and the home of the brave" is loosing its meaning rapidly and with a disturbing consistency. Because of the gross lack of heart felt repentance, I cannot help but believe the cry of "God Bless America" is falling on deaf ears as we have failed, by obedience, to show gratitude for past blessing. In spite of this we daily enjoy a multitude of God's blessings that sustains our existence and lives. The church world also is having problems of its own with the steady encroachment of sin based on stupidity within its own ranks.

The civil leaders hold an untold amount of meetings and discussions concerning the problems of America without any solutions forthcoming, because, having excommunicating God, they don't have any. Each political party blames the other; they rail on each other casting accusations back and forth, magnifying and creating more problems, and the solution continues to be as allusive as ever, simply because God remains continually and ignorantly rejected, and **"the truth continues to be held in unrighteousness"**. The blind leaders insist on remaining blind and the blind followers insist on blindly and ignorantly following them, both falling into the ditch of destruction, **[Matthew 15:14; Luke 6:39]**.

How appropriate are William Shakespeare's words **"What fools ye mortals be"**. **[Proverbs 1:7; 5:12-14], "The fear of the Lord is the beginning of knowledge: but fools despise wisdom and instruction. How have I hated instruction and my heart despised reproof; and have not obeyed the voice of my teachers, nor inclined my ear to them that instructed me! I was almost in all evil in the midst of the congregation and assembly".** Indeed William, we mortals do have a great propensity for foolishness, etc, etc, etc.

"BUT GOD, this great creative, loving, intervening God, who is rich in mercy, for his great love wherewith he loved us, Even when we were dead in sins, hath quickened us together with Christ, [by grace are ye saved;] And hath raised us up together, and made us sit together in heavenly places in Christ Jesus: That in ages to come he might show the exceeding riches of his grace in his kindness toward us through Christ Jesus. For by grace are ye saved through faith; and that not of yourselves: it is the gift of God: Not of works lest any man should boast. For we are his workmanship, created in Christ Jesus unto good works, which God hath before ordained that we should walk in them", [Ephesians 2: 4-10]. Thank you Jesus for the exceptions and making it possible for whosoever will, to be exceptions: to be delivered from the foolishness of this world of sin and stupidity.

Let me share a definition of stupidity I heard recently from a friend: STUPIDITY: Doing the same stupid thing over and over, hoping for better results each time you do it. When I heard that I was taken at how perfectly it fit sin, sin being the height of stupidity. Consequently, people wallow in sin and can't understand that it is they themselves; not God, who is the reason for all their continuing problems. Yet we still hear, "I just don't know how a loving God could allow this to happen". I will never cease to be amazed at how stupid supposedly intelligent people can be!

Coming into a reasoning relationship with God is simply to study his word and blending your life into it. This includes delighting in it, loving it, reading it, hearing it, studying it, practicing it, and DOING IT. This will promote the reasonable, intelligent conduct and construction of Godly activities and guarding against the unintelligent, unreasonable action of the *imposed impulses* which we see today in our world issuing death from *un-kept hearts.* This is the process of the renewing of the mind in God's counsel that will condition the mind, often referred to as the heart, in leading and controlling the conduct in Godly service, as unto the Lord.

There is in the thought of renewing of the mind, the reconstruction of the mind, etc, that suggests a breakdown in the process of teaching children from infancy, the attitudes and thinking that will contribute to the *God intended behavior that will be characteristic of these infants becoming little children, to older children, then into their teenage years and on to adulthood.* At this point in life, if their parents have fulfilled their God ordained duties and responsibilities toward them, they should be prepared to **"choose life so that both they and their seed may live, [Deuteronomy 30:19].** If they are not prepared, is it because their parents have chosen rather than life and blessing based on obedience for themselves and their children, death and cursing based on disobedience in opposition to God's will and counsel?

These little ones are not in a position in their formative, learning years to *"keep their heart with all diligence"*, realizing that out of these properly kept, guarded, Biblically trained, Holy Spirit taught hearts flow the issues of life. It is up to the parents to initiate this principle along with all the other contributing principles that apply. If their parents were not taught this, then we have a condition where a drastic renewal of the parental mind is needed, and if there are already little children involved, needed in a hurry. This would be an intelligent, wise choice.

The fear, reverence, of the Lord is still the beginning of wisdom and knowledge, but unfortunately, fools continue to despise wisdom and instruction which constitutes the **[Deuteronomy 30:19]** choosing of death and cursing which are also passed on to their "seed". Consequently, the deterioration of humanity continues with ever increasing speed, intensity, and ferocity.

[Hosea 4: 6-7], "My people are destroyed for lack of knowledge: because [as fools] thou hast rejected knowledge, I will also reject thee that thou shalt be no priest [Revelation 1:5-6] to me: seeing as thou hast forgotten the law [word] of thy God, I will also forget thy children. As they increased, so they sinned against me". Therefore, sin and iniquity has, and is increasing at an astounding rate and our government tells us that the solution; which is only available through the **Church of Jesus Christ, [Matthew 16:18]** is unconstitutional and cannot be presented to the public in an acceptable manner. So the nations are sacrificed to the gods of ignorance and stupidity where the blind leaders, with their willing deceived followers, all being fools, worship.

So the fools of **[Proverbs 1: 7]** continue to despise wisdom, knowledge, and instruction and the moral fiber of the nation continues to unravel and her people continue to be destroyed because they are denied the knowledge that they need to prevent destruction, **[Hosea 4: 6]**. Not only are they denied the knowledge in the public forum, but neither are they encouraged by their civil leaders to pursue it on a private level.

There is a discrepancy in this area concerning the encouraging and urging of the general populace to in-depth study of God's word existing among some of our spiritual leaders as well; some, thank God, not all. So as time marches on, we see a smaller percentage of the populace responding to Godly wisdom, counsel, and Biblical reasoned instruction, and a larger percentage reacting to the imposed impulses of sin and doing things that even by past worldly standards were absolutely idiotic, stupid, and utterly repulsive, but are becoming more acceptable day by day, even in some churches. Humanity continues to play out a scenario described, once again by our old friend, William Shakespeare as **"a tale told by an idiot, full of sound and fury and signifying nothing"**. Unfortunately, some of these repulsive things are becoming acceptable in even some of what used to be recognized and known as "churches".

And so, neither is the church world immune to this invasion of idiocy. Though the command of keeping the heart with all diligence is primarily to the church, I'm afraid it is not taken as seriously as it should be and the results are apparent. This applies as well to the civil leaders and their God ordained duties and responsibilities to the nations over which they are permitted to have leadership authority. We may well see **[Hosea 4: 6-7]** fitting in here and applying quite accurately, and in some cases, graphically. Civil leadership is not exempt from Godly spiritual leadership regardless of their foolish attempts to constitutionally dodge these duties and responsibilities. Yes William, the mortals continue to be fools every bit as much, and more, in our post-modern world as they were in your time. They have had more time and opportunity to become inventors of evil things and have taken full advantage of it and the snowball of sin continues to roll downhill and get larger as it rolls and little to nothing is being done in our governmental institutions to stop it, nor encourage the stopping of it.

By stifling the gospel of Jesus Christ, they are in fact encouraging, condoning, and promoting the enlarging of the snowball, and then have the audacity to ask God to bless such impudence when they should be hanging their heads in repentance for such shameful performances of their leadership duties. **[Matthew 12:30], "He that is not with me is against me; and he that gathereth not with me, scattereth abroad. [Romans 8: 6-9], "For to be carnally minded is death; but to be spiritually minded is life and peace. Because the carnal mind is enmity against God: for it is not subject to God, neither indeed can be. So then they that are in the flesh cannot please God. But ye are not in the flesh, but in the Spirit, if so be that the Spirit of God dwell in you.** *Now if any man have not the Spirit of Christ, he is none of his"*.

God help us to provide better examples for our children, teaching them diligently in word and deed about the wonders, majesty, love, glory, and power of this majestic, creative God who made us in his image and likeness so that we might have eternal intimate fellowship with him, enjoying the wonders and glories he has prepared for us. May God forgive us for our shortcomings and iniquity. Thank you Father for your love, mercy, grace, and much needed forgiveness. It is good to be forgiven, it is better and best, to "turn from our wicked ways", our faults, stupidity, and shortcomings to practice obedience in pleasing God, so that consistent forgiveness for such idiocy is not required. Assist us, Oh Lord, in heart felt repentance of our many and varied transgressions, enabling us to be a blessing to you and to each other as you administer your abundance of all things. **To you be all glory, honour, and praise forever and ever, Amen.**

[Deuteronomy 4: 4-9], verse 9, "Only take heed to thyself and keep thy soul diligently, lest thou forget the things which thine eyes have seen, and lest they depart from thy heart all the days of thy life: *but teach them to thy sons and to thy sons' sons"*. [6: 6-7], "And these words, which I command thee this day, shall be in thy heart: And thou shalt teach them *diligently* unto thy children, and shalt talk of them when thou sittest in thine house, and when thou walkest by the way, and when thou liest down and when thou risest up". [11: 13-17; 18-19], "And it shall come to pass, IF ye shall hearken diligently unto the commandments which I command you this day, *to love the Lord your God, and to serve him with all your heart and with all your soul".* Read and study vss, 14- 17 to get a better understanding of the results of disobedience to this with more graphic results found in **[Deuteronomy 28: 15-47].** Now let's return to **verse 18-19,** "Therefore shall ye lay up these my words in your heart and in your soul, and** [my translation], *station them at the entrance to your being; your heart, your mind, your soul, your spirit, that they become the abundance of the thoughts and intents of your heart controlling your conversation, conduct, and ways,* And ye shall teach them to your children, speaking of them when thou sittest in thine house, and when thou walkest by the way, when thou liest down, and when thou risest up".** Verse 20, once again, station them at the entrance to your being, making them the thoughts and intents of your heart and life. Now let's look at some results of all this, **verse 21, "That your days may be multiplied, and the days of your children, in the land which** [my translation]

I have given to you and have established by my providence for your well being and prosperity, *as the days of heaven upon the earth"*.

It is a sad thing that we intelligent human beings cannot seem to comprehend the value and blessings of diligent, willing obedience to the Lord that would enable us to enjoy a little of heaven on this earth. We seem to be incapable of expanding our minds to grasp the greatness and majesty of God in his relationship to us in what he wants to do for us, if we will just learn to be obedient, **"stirring up ourselves to take hold of God and serving the Lord thy God with joyfulness and gladness of heart for the abundance of all things"**. Unfortunately, for some Christians, just attending church and Sunday school seems to be the sum total of being obedient to the Lord; after all if you are saved by grace what else could possibly be required?

It is certainly conceivable that the non-Christian would not be aware of these things, but the Christian who have the word of God as their textbook of life; why are they so unaware of these **"things that accompany salvation", [Hebrews 6: 9] and diligently practicing them?** It is true that there is a lack of teaching in this area, but what prevents the individual from opening their Bible up, studying and digging these things out for themselves, being what I refer to as "self feeders"? After all, we do have the Holy Spirit as our teacher and councilor, **[John 14: 26]**, **"But the Comforter, which is the Holy Ghost, whom the Father will send in my name, he shall teach you all things, and bring all things to your remembrance, whatsoever I have said unto you"**, to assist us in attaining the essential knowledge that will prevent our destruction.

I do not know why there is not more emphasis put on these **"things" that accompany salvation"** and **"doing always** those "things" that please God", [John 8: 29]. Perhaps there is to much study required in ferreting these "things" out, and the challenge to apply them once they are found. Then another question arises; would we even recognize them as the **"things"** required when we ran across them in our studies, or have we even lost the common sense and intelligence needed for such recognition? **"Much study being a weariness to the flesh", [Ecclesiastes 12: 12]** certainly gives us a clue as to why humanity would shy away from the effort involved and required. Not having a **"vision of the value"** of such essential knowledge that tends to prevent destruction, **[Hosea 4: 6];** man with his undisciplined, non-Bible orientated and uneducated mind, naturally opts for the stuff, junk, fun and games of this world and the no-brainer pleasures they offer. [Isaiah 5: 24], **"Therefore as the fire devoureth the stubble, and the flame consumeth the chaff, so their root shall be as rottenness, and their blossom shall go up as dust: because they have cast away the law of the Lord of hosts, and despised the word of the Holy One of Israel".**

NOTES

NOTES

IV.   JUDGEMENTS

There has been, as of late, a considerable concern about people "judging" or simply making judgments concerning a multitude of things that are just a part of life and living. However, how do you discriminate between people who do not make proper, intelligent judgments concerning **[Matthew 7:20], "Wherefore by their fruits "lifestyle" ye shall know them"**, whether for right or wrong, good or evil, and those who become concerned enough about the evil fruit that is manifesting itself in such an abundance in our post-modern days to discuss these conditions and try to find solutions to the problems? This is going to necessitate a certain amount of, "judging" in order to determine and establish such solutions. We can only hope that such judging will be tempered with Godly wisdom, knowledge, understanding, intelligence, and common sense.

Unfortunately there is a scripture that has been misused, abused, and wrongly presented that has created much confusion among the Christian community and has created much spiritual bondage with people afraid to make "judgments" about anything for fear of being Biblically incorrect. That scripture is **[Matthew 7: 1], "Judge not, that ye be not judged"**.

It is left hanging there with no explanation for understanding of its meaning, but places Christians under condemnation, depending on how they have been taught, if they should happen to make a judgment on some issue or a person who has not learned to **"possess their vessel "exercise their life" with honor", [1 Thessalonians 4: 4].** These are situations and conditions wherein judgments must be made for proper Bible based conditions to prevail. Judges, Old Testament, New

Testament, and modern day judges were established just for the purpose of "judging". Whether the judging was done with Biblical understanding, wisdom, knowledge, and competence is, of course another matter about which judgments must be made from time to time.

We cannot live without judging, or making judgments, which are nothing more than making choices and properly discriminating between one thing or person and another. Wisdom and understanding are essentials in the matter of judging and we are admonished in **[Psalms 119: 104; Proverbs 4: 5-7], "Get wisdom, get understanding: forget it not; neither decline from the words of my mouth. Forsake her not, and she shall reserve thee: love her and she shall keep thee. Wisdom is the principle thing; therefore get wisdom: and with all thy getting get understanding"**. It is important that we get a Biblical understanding of this misused scripture, and we can move in that direction by a close look at **[Matthew 7: 2], "For with what judgment ye judge, ye shall be judged: and with what measure ye mete, it shall be measured to you again"**. This does not do away with judging, but gives us some very essential instruction of what basis to make our judgments so they will be made properly. They are to made with Godly wisdom, knowledge, understanding, intelligently, and with common sense and discretion; not foolishly, indiscriminately, and without the required essentials just listed for properly executing such judgments.

[Galatians 6: 1], "Brethren, if a man be overtaken in a fault, *ye which are spiritual,* restore such and one in the spirit of meekness; considering thyself, lest thou also be tempted". Here a judgment is to be made concerning a brother for whatever reason it might be, but it is to be done by spiritually mature brethren in a spirit of meekness, certainly with concern, compassion, love, and understanding; but with firmness, if that is warranted. Immature brethren, though sincere, may well lack the knowledge and experience needed for such a task and make a judgment based on personal feelings and emotions rather than Biblical discretion.

There is a difference between talking for the purpose of gossip and seriously discussing existing situations and conditions because you are concerned enough to search for, and get involved in the solutions to problems rather than being just another contributor to the problems. Let us bear in mind; there are solutions, or should I rather say, A Solution, with His prescribed mentality resulting in the appropriate thinking, **[Isaiah 55:8-9],** thoughts, and conduct, [lifestyles]. This "solution", which when intelligently applied and adhered to will be a manifestation of the desperately needed solution to humanities troubles and ever increasing dilemma's that man seems so insistent and determined to ignorantly heap upon himself.

Whether we pursue and apply this process of deliverance or not, or even care, is another question. Of course to apply this process we would first have to know, or at least have an idea, of what things it might include and consist of, and have the discriminating intelligence to know the Biblical alternative to "judge" between right and wrong and the courage to apply that which is correct. If they, the Christian community, do know and manifest these Biblical prerogatives in whatever way they choose in order to be affective, you can pretty well be assured that there is a segment of society who will be offended by it, or especially by the Biblical direction and the religious motives for doing it. And of course that is the great sin of society in our post-modern America today, the offending of someone, unless of course, that someone is a Christian, in which case it seems to be open season.

However, it was not always this way in America, nor will it remain this way. Regardless of the worldly opinions about God, his Christ, and his people; the world with its contrary opinions, attitudes, and practices is a lost cause. Due to Biblical information, we are able to thus make proper God ordained decisions and judgments. **[John 17:17], "Sanctify them through thy truth: thy word is truth".**

[James 4:17] "Therefore to him that knoweth to do good, and doeth it not; to him it is sin", or to be precise, the production of "evil fruit". According to **[Ephesians 1:1-3]** we all in our own time, belonged to an evil fruit producing class of people and we know, if we are honest with ourselves, that we have the propensity to revert back to that if we don't stay in the word of God and **[Proverbs 4:] "Keep your [our own] heart with all diligence; for out of it come the issues of life". To pursue this should be our ultimate priority.** To do this we will find it necessary to make some "judgments" concerning individuals we are to stay separated from as habitual friends and companions, **[1Corinthians 15: 33], "Be not deceived: evil communications corrupt good manners". [2 Corinthians 6: 14-18],** Read, study, and meditate on this and see if you can find some essential reasons to make judgments as to people and conditions. Many are the marriages and lives that have been ruined because Bible directed discriminating judgments were ignored. Many are the lives that have been destroyed because impressionable young people started "hanging with the wrong crowd" and had not learned to judge that, and those, with which they were in contact with wisdom, knowledge, and understanding.

This involves a life-time of continual mind renewal by increased Bible input and knowledge, basically referred to as "study" which is where we lose many as **[Ecclesiastes 12:12]** tells us that **"much study is a weariness to the flesh"** and the inherent laziness of the general populace in the pursuit and study of Biblical truths seems to kick in about here. The producing of evil fruit is not an "issue of life", but rather an issue of death that proceeds from the heart and functions by worldly standards, un-kept and unguarded by the neglect of **[Psalms 1:2], "delighting in and meditation on the word of God"**, a process of **the [Romans 12:2] "escaping conformity to this world by being transformed "from death unto life", [John 5: 24], through the "renewing of the mind" from worldliness to Godliness, from walking after the flesh to walking in the Spirit, [Romans 8: 1].**

If we are not allowed to make intelligent "Biblical taught judgments" concerning the evil "fruit" of this world, how are we going to be able to successfully combat it? There is undoubtedly an intelligent application of "judging" versus an indiscriminate, unintelligent, judging by people **[2 Peter 2:12] "as brute beasts, who speak evil [or make judgments] of the things that they understand not; and shall utterly perish in their own corruption". [Proverbs 4: 7] "With all thy getting, get understanding".** To be forbidden to make intelligent Biblically informed judgments between right and wrong is to give Satan place and an advantage, **[2 Corinthians: 11].**

We have a nation, indeed a world full of "natural brute beasts" who speak evil of God and his goodness, who have a total lack of understanding of God, his goodness and fullness and couldn't care less. They only have to open their mouths to expose their ignorance, and are ignorant of the fact they are exposing such ignorance; nor are they intelligent enough to even care or be embarrassed concerning their ignorance of spiritual matters that they so ignorantly attempt to express knowledgeable opinions on.

They can criticize and denounce that of which they have no knowledge: they cannot however, with their lack of knowledge of God and his Word, express intelligent ideas and opinions nor make sound judgments concerning these spiritual matters. These are among those **"who darkeneth counsel by words without knowledge", [Job 38:2].**

They have absolutely no concept of the importance and value of these Biblical principles in the makeup and establishment of productive lives that is taught in **[Matthew 12:35]; "A good man out of the good treasure of the heart bringeth forth good things", or "good fruit".**

The "brute beasts" however, exist in opposition to God and practice their [2 Peter 2:2] "pernicious ways; by reason of whom the ways of truth are evil spoken of" and by their "pernicious ways" deceive many; thus do the blind lead the blind unto destruction, [Luke 6:39]. These "brute beasts" lack the discriminating intelligence to know or even show concern for what these "good" things of God's provision and abundance are; nor do they understand the value of them. They do, however, enjoy them every day of their lives without realizing or recognizing the source of them. These are the ones who as evil men, out of the abundance of evil hearts bring forth evil things and have been allowed to set non-Biblical policy for our nation and her people and force recognition and accepting of it. Christians must possess the wisdom, knowledge, and understanding, to make discriminating judgments concerning who these "brute beasts" are, and be able to make those judgments without coming under *ecclesiastical sanctions* for such judgments. **[Matthew 7: 15-21]**, gives us good Bible counsel for making proper judgments, **verse 20, "Wherefore by their fruits,** lifestyle, **ye shall know them".**

The lack of perception and understanding of the value of these Biblically presented and taught principles and absolutes is sadly and unfortunately shared to a certain degree among many of those within the professing Christian family. These fail to avail themselves of the depth of God's word **by [Psalms 1:2; 2 Timothy 2:15] delighting in, and intense meditation and study to search out and [Proverbs 4:7] get understanding of these "things that please God and accompany salvation" [John 8:29; Hebrews 6:9].**

Contrary to man's thinking and thoughts and the resultant conclusions of his erroneous concepts, there is still only one way to heaven; and God's provision of Jesus by way of the cross is it. **[John 14:6], "Jesus saith unto him, I am the way, the truth, and the life: no man cometh to the Father, but by me".**

There is no such thing as "many roads to heaven" as is claimed by the spiritually ignorant. Our constitution may allow for the erroneous "freedom of religion", *but God makes no allowances for it whatsoever, and this world is going to realize, to late, that God's opinion is the only one that counts.* **[John 10]** gives an extremely good and accurate accounting of this. Study it thoroughly, prayerfully, and meditatively.

This is not a judgment I have made, but a fact and Biblical principle that God has set in place. My position is that I am very much in total agreement with him. The Bible does not teach nor allow for "freedom of religion" as is claimed by those who are enslaved and operate within the wisdom of this world who **"are destroyed for lack of knowledge", [Hosea 4:6].** As Christians, following Bible counsel and commandments, we must not only be allowed to, but encouraged to make *Biblically based* discernments, discriminations, and judgments of these things, otherwise we give place to the devil without even being aware of it and we all suffer because of it. Thus his advantage over us continues to increase while we sit in frustration wondering what's happening and why. By this time, however, we should be well aware of what is happening and how it has come to be. Because of the varied ideas of relativity and indiscriminate tolerance, and thoughts regarding a solution to the problems, a solution may be somewhat obscured; however, with Bible orientation and counsel it shouldn't be to difficult to find, if we have the courage to do so and express it.

Basically what has happened is that the Christian community has done the same thing Adam did. We've abdicated our authority and dominion position and allowed those opposed to the righteous principles and counsel of God's Word of truth and deliverance to take over, make the rules and set the standards for the battle instead of initiating and exercising God's rules, **[2 Corinthians 10:4]**. We have allowed our ability to use the **[Ephesians 6:17] "sword of the spirit"** to become dull and ineffective through lack of personal care, use, study, and practice with it. In affect we have been the ones responsible for allowing the erecting of some "gates of hell" by way of our abdication through neglect, and we don't exercise our authority for fear of "offending" someone and being penalized for it.

I am beginning to wonder if the church even knows what that dominion authority, **[Genesis 1:26]**, consists of that was originally designed in man and intended to produce by way of God's "image and likeness". [Isaiah 26:9-10], **"With my soul have I desired thee in the night; yea with my spirit within me will I seek thee early; for when thy "judgments" are in the earth, [and in operation], [THEN] the inhabitants of the world will learn righteousness; [but not until then]. Let favour be shewed to the wicked, yet he will not learn righteousness; in the land of uprightness will he deal** unjustly, and will not behold the majesty of the Lord. [Isaiah 32:6], "For the vile person will speak villainy, and his heart will work iniquity, to practice hypocrisy, and to utter error against the Lord, to make empty the soul of the hungry, and will cause the drink of the thirsty to fail". We do have "brute beasts" dwelling among us, many of which are of *"our own countrymen"*, many in "high" places, erroneously referred to as "higher powers", **[Romans 13: 1]**.

The soul of America today is famished in its lack; it's being hungry and thirsty for the righteousness of the Lord. **[Amos 8: 11], "Behold, the days come, saith the Lord God, that I will send a famine in the land, not a famine of bread, nor a thirst for water, but of hearing the words of the Lord"**. This has come about by the "vile brute beast" persons who in their pseudo authority of leadership have "caused all America to sin" just as the vile, evil kings and leaders of Israel did in their history recorded in the Old Testament, from which we cannot seem to learn a thing. It is the "vile" who in their failure to initiate and administer correct leadership under Biblical principles of authority and leadership that have caused the degradation of our nation to take place, **[Proverbs 29:2], "When the righteous are in authority, the people rejoice: but when the wicked beareth rule, the people mourn"**.

There seems to be much more mourning than rejoicing going on in our nation and the world these days. We the people, on the other hand are not guiltless in this degrading process. **[Luke 12:48], "___For unto whom much is given, of him will much be required: and to whom men have committed much, of him they will ask the more"**. Though we have committed much to these leaders in the care of our entire nation and her people, we have not demanded much of them, but allow them to continue in their own "pernicious ways", deluded and deluding. Neither have we demanded much of ourselves in the matter of seeking, embracing, establishing, and practicing righteousness, **[Matthew 6: 33], [Acts 10: 34-35].**

Is this possibly because we have not demanded much in the way of righteousness and holiness of ourselves, and as a result the whole concept of God in his fullness, glory and majesty has diminished in our consciousness and **"the excellency that is in them goeth away, and they die, even without wisdom, [Job 4: 21].** It's an unfortunate thing that we find as Paul did that these "vile" persons were comprised mainly of his **"own countryman", [2 Corinthians 11:26; 1Thessalonians 2:14].**

We are seeing graphic examples of this today where citizenship means nothing to many who are loyal to some foreign, destructive ideology or religion and commit atrocities in and against this nation wherein they have their citizenship and may even have been born. Are we not allowed to make judgments in such cases as these for our own safety and preservation? Forget tolerance for such abomination and those who commit such things against decency, honor and God's goodness. Forget tolerance for such ideologies and religions that teach and promote such abominable things who destroy themselves and all who reject their erroneous teachings. Those who foster and promote such things must be held accountable; not only for doing such things but, even for the thoughts and thinking, the ideologies and concepts that produce such things. **[Ecclesiastes 8: 11], "Because sentence against an evil work is not executed speedily, therefore the hearts of the sons of men are fully set in them to do evil".**

The question is: who is, can, or will hold these "hijackers of humanity" accountable? Who has the authority, the right, the courage and backbone to assert themselves to such a task? Indeed, would such a person or people be restricted from such activities by some twisted applications of laws, rules, regulations, etc administered by the **"sleight of man and his cunning craftiness", [Ephesians 4: 14]**, thus destroying himself and his society? **[Proverbs 28: 4-5; 29: 2]**

We haven't seen any signs of any governmental agencies rise to the challenge, or those of our judicial system. Unfortunately they are not qualified to such an endeavor as to bring about the solutions, as they themselves are contributors to the problems in formulating rules, regulations, and laws in opposition against God and his word of counsel and correction; **[2 Corinthians 10:5],"Casting down imaginations, and every high thing that exalts itself against the knowledge of God, and bringing into captivity** *every thought,* **to the obedience of Christ".** It is from these thoughts, the intents and abundance of the heart and minds that these ways and conduct proceed: good unto good or evil unto evil.

We need an across the board of humanity, *renewing of the hearts and minds* that are of destructive, abominable practices, thoughts and ways; contrary to the righteousness, holiness, truth, and goodness that characterizes the divine nature of God. In spite of mans great achievements and accomplishments, in spite of all his institutions of higher education and his accumulations of scientific attainments, etc. etc.; idiocy, and stupidity remain among his leading characteristics and indeed may be the leading ones, proving his final undoing in his rebellion against his creator and his God, **[Romans 1:22], "Professing themselves to be wise they became fools".** [2 **Peter 3:9], "_____ For God is not willing that any should perish, but that all should come to repentance".**

Though a man may think his thoughts are good and correct, if they be thoughts causing confusion and destruction, he is an emissary of confusion and destruction. Whether or not his mindset and heart content are correct can only be determined by and from God's perspective, not mans, for man is inherently evil, and thus will decree his evil to be good, and whatever tends to correction of his erroneous ways to be evil. **[Isaiah 5:20], "Woe unto them that call good, and good evil; that put darkness for light, and light for darkness; that put bitter for sweet, and sweet for bitter".** Man without God is unknowledgeable and thus totally undependable in affairs of holiness and righteousness. That which is evil he calls good, and that which is good that threatens the evil he enjoys, he will call evil, **[Isaiah 5: 20]. [Genesis 6:5], "And God saw that the wickedness of man was great in the earth and that every imagination of his heart was only evil continually.** Man has proven himself to be totally ignorant and undependable in matters of "the things above", and not very intelligent concerning his handling of the "things here on earth".

[Ephesians 2: 4-10], "BUT GOD, _____: Whatever choices, decisions, or judgments man makes, he must depend on God's counsel for guidance and direction. Man's thinking and thoughts, thus his ways, apart from God's wisdom, counsel, and teachings, must for the well being of man, be thoroughly dismissed, and discarded, otherwise man deceives, deludes, and destroys himself, **[2 Timothy 3: 13; James 1: 22]**, and those that fall victim to the decisions and judgments that are a result of the mentality that is produced by such erroneous thinking and thoughts.

Only the gospel of Jesus Christ provides for such correct change and eventuality of well being through the transforming of the hearts and minds to the enriching of individuals and thus, cultures and nations. If its results we need; and it is, whether we want them or not is beside the point, our feelings don't count because they will invariably lead to misconduct, behavior contrary to God's counsel and righteousness. Only God's word is valid in this. We must **"stir up ourselves to take hold of**

God" [Isaiah 64:7], and embrace that which has proven itself to bring about those results which humanity is in such desperate need of that are a result of **[Ephesians 2: 10]; "For we are his workmanship, created in Christ Jesus unto good works, which God hath before ordained that we should walk in them".** This should be the ultimate goal in life for each and every one of us without exception, saint and sinner alike. It does seem, at times, to be a bit difficult to convince the saints of this, with the sinner having no idea or understanding of it whatsoever.

To the sinner, it starts with Jesus, to the saint, after having started with Jesus, it continues with Jesus as a lifetime journey of purpose and fulfillment. What do you want out of life for yourself and your loved ones, **[Deuteronomy 30:19], life and blessing with peace that passeth understanding [Philippians 4:7; Psalms 16:11] and fullness of joy,** or; contrary-wise **[Romans 6:23], "The wages of sin which is still death",** the survival with a miserable existence of strife and contention in this world, the pursuit and conclusion of which is eternal death. It would seem that a person endowed with at least a minimum level of intelligence, saint and sinner alike, would be able to observe the world around them and the abominations that are taking place daily in our own nation as well as the rest of the world and conjure up enough inspiration and intelligence to effect an upgrading unto Biblical principles for the enrichment of their own lives. There is room for this in all our lives, including my own.

Paul put it very well in **[Philippians 3:12-16], vs. 13-14, "Brethren, I count not myself to have apprehended: but this one thing I do, forgetting those things which are behind, and reaching forth unto those things which are before,** *I press toward the mark for the prize of the high calling of God in Christ Jesus"*.

Paul had many things in his past that consisted of some very painful, erroneous conduct that he, like all of us, need to repent of in order to be free, cleansed, and forgiven of if there is to be growth and development in becoming what God has planned for us if we are to be free from struggling under the weight of condemnation of those things. As God, through genuine repentance has forgiven us, we must forgive ourselves. Otherwise we will sit around and whine beneath a load of self imposed condemnation and self pity even after the garbage has been washed away by the blood of Jesus, **[Romans 8: 1]**.

So God provided a way of escape and deliverance from those things and the accusations that the devil keeps accusing the brethren of concerning those things. Paul met Jesus on the road to Damascus and was set free from sin and the condemnation of his past.

We all need at one time or another, the sooner the better, our own "Damascus road" encounter with Jesus in repenting and believing the gospel, and because of our propensity to evil, to remain in an attitude of the **"baptism of repentance"**.

This is not judging people, but judging sin which God has already condemned. This is *simply agreeing with the word of God;* it is just the way things have to be and *man's contrary opinions are worthless.* We need the Lord for the beginning and continuation of life and life more abundantly in all areas of our being, spiritual, psychological, physical, and material. Without the direct assistance of the Holy Spirit, the renewing of our minds becomes an impossibility in **[2 Corinthians 10:5]: "casting down [evil, vain] imaginations, and every high thing that exalts itself against the knowledge of God, and bringing into captivity every thought to the obedience of Christ"**.

There is no such thing as successfully resisting the devil unless it is preceded by a **"submitting of yourselves therefore to God", [James 4:7], a "repenting and believing the gospel", [Mark 1:15].** This implies believing the gospel *unto obedience,* not just accepting it as a good idea that ought to be considered whenever you find yourself in one of the foxholes of life, but obeyed when things are going good in order to please God. This should be your first desire and consideration to keep yourself and your descendents out of those foxholes; and as another consideration for thought and meditation. It shouldn't take a real deep understanding of life and it's complexities to figure this out. It does seem as though there are those who need a considerable amount of counsel and assistance in this area, as we all do from time to time to a certain extent; but that's only one of the areas of life where God's word is so necessary and applicable to all.

Somehow I knew there was a reason that God instructed us in **[Colossians 3:2] & [Psalms 1:2]** to **"Set our affection on things above and not on things on the earth" and to" Delight in his word and meditate in it day and night":** in order to establish a good abundance in our hearts, thus *displacing those things that are contrary to the gospel of Jesus Christ.* **[John 14:26], "But the Comforter, which is the Holy Ghost, whom the Father will send in my name, he shall teach you all things, and bring all things to your remembrance, whatsoever I have said unto you".**

Thank God for the Holy Spirit who is always on the job, teaching, reminding, training, etc; and we may not even be aware of his presence until all of a sudden there is a remembrance of something "out of the blue" that we hadn't even considered. Then we turn to our Bible to make sure we don't misstate it and sure enough, it's underlined; we've been there before; how many times, we don't know, but it fits here, so we are pleasantly reminded of it by our master teacher. It's an amazing thing, this grace of God, who because of his unconditional love, he applies constantly and so thoroughly in all areas of our lives to assist us and keep us on track for the pleasure, glory, and honor of God, and ultimately, for our own benefit and eternal prosperity.

NOTES

NOTES

V. BORN OR CREATED

Being created equal is not much to crow about considering the fact that all men are born sinners, **[Romans 3:23; Ephesians 2:1-3]** and the majority of them have remained so, **[Matthew 7:13]**. In consideration of man, I won't try to split hairs on the difference between being created or being born, as they both have to do with coming into being. Not being satisfied with this sinner business and seeing the devastating effects it has had, and is having on humanity, plus what I have personally experienced as a teenage idiot and beyond; the prospect of the continuing and final results of it helped persuade and motivate me to take advantage of the way of deliverance God **[Mark 1:15; John 3:16]** provided for me.

Over the multitude of years since I was a teenager indulging in an abundance of stupid things I formulated in my mind; yes, iniquity is found in us just like it was found in Lucifer, **[Ezekiel 28: 15]**. Since those teenage and "twenty" years, I have come to really enjoy a relationship of love with my Lord. It took much longer to develop this relationship than it should have even though I accepted Jesus as my saviour when I was thirteen. Yes, I went to church, yes I considered myself a Christian, yes, I still did some stupid things. Going to church didn't stop that nor did these things magically disappear upon my becoming a Christian and attending church like a good Christian boy should; nor did the desire for these things automatically go way. I knew some of these things were wrong even before accepting Jesus as Lord and Saviour. I have since come to realize that sin was not my problem; my stupidity and ignorance in indulgence was my problem. I had the knowledge, but I didn't conduct myself within it. That is stupidity, and from the apparent condition of our nation, we are still experiencing an abundance of it today in all areas of life.

Over the years through a Holy Spirit induced and developed intense love and desire to blend my life with God's Word I come to realize that a major part of receiving Jesus as Saviour was receiving Him as the living, revealed, cleansing Counsel and Word of God. I came, by way of some rather intense study, to realize that **"this thing of repentance and believing the gospel", [Mark 1: 15],** included love for, and obedience to this glorious gospel of life and deliverance from sin and definitely included *my decision,* prompted of course by the Holy Spirit; I still had to make the decision, just as you do, to **"turn from *my* wicked ways", [2 Chronicles 7: 14].** Now the majority of these ways though not major transgressions of God's will, design, and purpose of God's counsel were nevertheless **"things that were displeasing to Him", [John 8: 28],** and as such needed to be *"weeded out and destroyed",* opting for an enriched relationship of love and obedience to God with Jesus as the perfect example of this.

These "wicked ways" and the lesser things that were, as a child of God, still displeasing to him were results of wrong thinking and thoughts, attitude, abundance of heart; all products of a mind that still needed some intensive **"renewing"** which was, due to my former worldly conditioning, going to take some time of re-creating which God was already, **[Revelation 4: 11]** in the process of doing. **"This beautiful Holy Spirit, sent from God to teach me all things and bring all things to remembrance, [John 14: 26[, that I needed for development and maturing as a Christian was already patiently working on me"**. The process of re-creation was already underway.

It didn't take much intelligence to figure out that life was far better than death, light was far superior to darkness, hope and peace was much more desirable than hopelessness and despair, and joy and happiness was to be preferred to brokenness, distress, and sadness with a considerable amount of anxiety thrown in from time to time for good measure. I'm fairly well convinced that a good percentage of people, if they put some effort into it, could come to this same conclusion. However to follow thru on that conclusion could prove a bit difficult with all the distractions that ambush us with a disturbing degree of regularity. That does present a challenge many are not willing to face, but face they must for the solutions needed to their problems.

Experience on both sides of the fence, as a sinner or as a saint concerning these things, can teach volumes if a **person has eyes to see, ears to hear, [Matthew 11:14]: [Matthew 13:15], and a mentality that has been conditioned to learn, comprehend, and understand with, [Proverbs 1:7]. The renewing of the mind, [Romans 12:2], is essential to this.** Unfortunately an attitude such as this concerning Biblically taught and induced spiritual matters is extremely rare in the unsaved populace; not being quite so rare in the redeemed community of Christ, but still wanting in to many instances. Thus do problems arise and at times cause havoc among the saints. This is also stupidity of indulgence with things, thoughts, and ways that ought not so to be. **[Hosea 4: 6-7]** and **[Job 5: 7]** put in their appearance here.

So it was, that with considerable consideration of a need for a change in life, a little prompting from my Mother, reinforced by parent's prayers, very little contributing of intelligence from myself, I accepted Jesus Christ as my Lord and Saviour, all of this being orchestrated, unknown to me at the time, by the Holy Spirit. This I was to really realize later, with some additional, slow to be accumulated, intelligence, and some additional erroneous experience, that this was the only way man could possibly escape his sinful nature and the ensuing penalties for such foolishness, **[John 14:6; Acts 4:10-12]**.

So, armed with Mom's urging, considerable desperation and need for positive change, and as yet a very small showing of intelligence, I chose to avail myself of that which God, because of his love, has made available through Jesus Christ to all mankind, **[Deuteronomy 30: 19-20]** of salvation **[2 Corinthians 5:17-19], and reconciliation back to himself.**

Since entering into this realm of God's kingdom **[Matthew 6:33; Mark 1:15] through repentance of sin, believing the gospel and learning to serve the Lord thy God with joyfulness and gladness of heart for the abundance of all things, [Deuteronomy 28:47], God has proven his faithfulness, [2 Timothy 2:13], and his love over and over again.** What a wonderful experience to be enabled to rise above the darkness and desperation of the sin of this world and enter into the light and life of the kingdom of God **unto righteousness, peace and holiness, [Hebrews 12:14], being partakers of God's divine nature, [2 Peter 1:4].**

How good it is for brethren to dwell together in unity, [Psalms 133:1], and be seated together in heavenly places in Christ Jesus, [Ephesians 2:6]. That is a glorious equality to be desired and attained to that projects one unto additional intelligence and a host of other rewards and benefits that begins with **[Psalms 111:10; Proverbs 1:7; 4:7; 9:10], fearing, reverencing, God and submitting to his will and ways, [James 4:7; Isaiah 55:7-9]. This is all based on accepting Jesus Christ as Lord, Saviour, and King, for life and eternity, [2 Timothy 3:16].**

This book is definitely not dedicated to the proposition that all men are created equal, but to the proposition that contained in the **initial creation of all men was the image and likeness of God, [Genesis 1: 26],** and that this level of equality of **"the excellency that is in them" [Job 4:21], can be resurrected in the hearts, minds, souls, and spirit of men, [2 Corinthians 5:17].** From this point on, **"in him we live and move and have our being", [Acts 17:28].** This is to be accomplished by repenting of our miserable lot of sin **"and the iniquity that is found in thee", [Ezekiel 28:15]** and embracing the gospel of God unto life everlasting.

This continues on with the willing, diligent, obedience of studying, learning, and doing, [2 Timothy 2:15; Matthew 11:29; James 1:22], "always those things that please him", [John 8:29]: the whole counsel of God unto his glory, honour, praise and pleasure, [Revelation 4:11].

Let us join together in Christ and pursue with renewed enthusiasm, wisdom, knowledge, understanding, intelligence, and common sense, these truths and absolutes of redemption and reconciliation for all men everywhere. **This truth, [John 8:32] and absolutes, that makes men and nations free from the bondage and slavery of sin will do us good in providing the knowledge that is essential to the prevention of destruction, [Hosea 4:6]. This will secure the temporal and eternal well being of those and their "seed" upon condition of choosing life and blessing rather than death and cursing, [Deuteronomy 30:19].** Unto this we were born, created, and called. This is our reason and purpose for being. [1 Corinthians 10: 31], **"Whether therefore ye eat or drink, or whatsoever ye do, do all to the glory of God".**

NOTES

VI. BENEFITS AND REWARDS

[Psalms 103: 2]: "Bless the Lord, O my soul and forget not all his *benefits*." [Hebrews 11: 6]: "But without faith it is impossible to please Him [God]: for he that cometh to him must believe that He is and that He is a *rewarder* of them that *diligently* seek Him."

Before we can forget, or rather remember, all his benefits, we need to know what they are, which may require a rather intensive and extended time of study. This however, is to be accomplished over the period of what we would consider as a "lifetime". But to begin with let's take a look at the primary ones that are available just for the asking when we are still ignorant of any of the others.

The provision and opportunity of **"repentance"** is not only a **benefit,** but a **requirement** before any of the rest can be received. I refer to "repentance" as a provision, because it is given by the God who wishes above all else to **"forgive"** your sins and reconcile you back into a pre-sin relationship with himself. I refer to "repentance" as an opportunity, as this is something we can and must contribute to the establishing of this relationship or there can be no relationship. It is a foundational requirement immediately followed by **[Mark 1: 15], believing in the Gospel of Jesus Christ.** The implication given here is, **[believing],** not to simple acknowledgement of an existence of Jesus Christ, but **[believing unto obedience].**

An example of this obedience is given in **[John 4: 34],** and gives us valuable insight into the attitude of service we must seek to develop; **"Jesus saith unto them, my meat is to do the will of Him that sent me and to finish his work".** The word "meat" here represents the whole sustenance and object of his being, his whole purpose, **to do his Father's will.**

Another example we find in **[John 8: 29]** is a promise of the reward of God's continual presence, a combination of benefits and rewards **"for doing always those things that *please* Him."** This is made possible by **[Psalms 119: 165],** developing **"a love for God's Word".** You have to see, get a concept or vision of the immense value of it, **"delight in it, and meditate on it day and night", [Psalms 1: 2].** It is at this juncture you begin to really get an understanding and knowledge of the importance of the Word and the benefits and rewards that are a result of being obedient to it. How wonderful it would be if we all learned this early on in life so we might indeed enjoy life to its fullest, **"seated together in heavenly places with Christ", [Ephesians 2: 6].** This must integrated into our daily living so as to become our lifestyle with diligent study and practice.

Too often people are invited to accept Jesus Christ as Saviour and Lord without ever understanding that the prerequisite and initial beginning of this is **[repentance of sin]**, nor do they really understand the concept or the gravity concerning the need of it, so they accept Jesus, neglect real soul depth repentance, and bring their garbage of sin into the family of God. Somehow they have been fed the idea that this is all covered by **[grace]** and the necessity for obedience is put on the back burner neglected and often forgotten or never really taken seriously. Once again we are reminded that **[Hosea 4: 7],** gives us a principle that is set in place, **"_____ seeing thou hast forgotten the law of thy God, I will also forget thy children". [Isaiah 5:24], "_____and their blossom "children, seed, posterity, descendents, shall go up as dust, blown and carried away in the storms of their iniquities that are found in them".** Excuse the Edwards spin I put on this: I find it to be born out by scripture itself and fits in very nicely.

Repentance of sin is provided to enable us to leave the sinfulness of our former existence in the place it originated, never to be burdened by it again. That doesn't mean we won't be bothered by temptation to return to it. Grace now comes to the surface and does its work: if we stumble and fall. **[1 John 2:1-2]** comes into focus, **"My little children, these things I write unto you, that ye sin not.** But, however, nevertheless, **"if any man sin, we have an advocate with the Father, Jesus Christ the righteous: And he is the propitiation for our sins: and not for ours only, but also for the sins of the whole world."**

Now we begin to see the need for the **"baptism of repentance" [John 1:4; Luke 3:3],** a continual realization of our propensity to sin, but God's provision of continual cleansing through *repentance and obedience on our part, grace and forgiveness on his part.* Our part includes diligent study of God's Word. **[John 15:3], "Now ye are clean through the "applied" word that I have spoken unto you"**. **"Applied" "being a doer of the word and not hearers only", [James 1: 22] implies "obedience"**, just in case you failed to pick up on that. Don't be concerned about God taking care of his part; zero in on your part and work at perfecting it. God took care of his part in **[John 3: 16]**, once and for all, and is still **"a rewarder of those who diligently seek him"**.

Now we see the benefits of **the command and opportunity to repent, forgiveness being based on genuine repentance with grace to sustain us if we fall and an advocate, Jesus Christ the righteous as our advocate before God for continued restoration and development in our walk with the Lord led by the counsel of the Word as taught by the Holy**

Spirit. There are additional things we will see and enjoy as benefits and rewards during our personal maturing process in spiritual growth.

Be diligent, be patient: **[1 Peter 5: 8]: "Be sober, be vigilant; because your adversary the devil, as a roaring lion walketh about seeking whom he may devour."** In the case of Christians, **[2 Corinthians 5: 17]**, new creations in Christ who have been delivered from his jaws of death; it is a matter of being "re-devoured" or going back into sin and iniquity. The scriptures have some very quaint comments about this in describing God's attitude toward sin and the person who thus indulges themselves, having once been delivered from them.

[Proverbs 26: 11], "As a dog returneth to his vomit, so a fool returneth to his folly. [2 Peter 2: 19-22], note verse 22; **"But it has happened to them according to the true proverb. The dog is returned to his own vomit again; and the sow that was washed to her wallowing in the mire."** This gives a rather graphic accounting of the Biblical view of what the church so glibly refers to as "backsliding". It would seem to have much more serious eternal implications than the simple term "backsliding" implies.

The graphics of this truth with its implications is revealed to those individuals who take the time to study, to examine themselves for correction and growth in the family of God. They prefer their meat, their sustenance to be a diet of doing the Fathers will and pleasing Him with such conduct and behavior, **[John 4: 34]**, rather than **[Psalms 1:1], "walking in the counsel of the ungodly, standing in the way of sinners, and sitting in the seat of the scorners,"** thus feasting on the **"vomit of sin and iniquity and the folly of fools".**

This being "re-devoured" by the devil when through Jesus Christ we have been given authority and dominion over him, and can control the situation, is absolutely senseless. The vast majority of us have had a run at this and failed but that is part of learning, if indeed we did learn anything, which at times does seem to pose a bit of a question. Some never seem to learn, but most of us will spend a lifetime at it and still have a few difficulties along the way. Theirs will be the difficulties of learning and conforming to the truth of God's divine counsel, not the difficulties of suffering from the idiocy of continual transgressions, **[Romans 8: 1-8]**.

This is where God's sustaining grace is so important; stabilizing us while we get things straightened out and remaining afterwards, which seems to be kind of an ongoing process. It is important that we realize as Paul did, that God's grace is sufficient for us to take us through our trials and tribulations which will invariably arise. **[Hosea 5: 6-7], "Although affliction cometh not forth of the dust, neither doth trouble spring out of the ground; yet man is born unto trouble as the sparks fly upward."**

Some of these **"afflictions"** are created by our own stupidity, some by the stupidity of others, and some just seem to happen: all however, through the stupidity of sin somewhere along the road of spiritual growth and development. But through it all; God's grace is still sufficient, but was never intended to cover man's willful disobedience and rebellion. Repentance and forgiveness was provided for that purpose.

This stain of disobedience we must clean up ourselves, **"stirring up ourselves to take hold of God", [Isaiah 64: 7]**, although God is ready to assist us when we ask, and ask we must, for we cannot do it without Him. Some have tried, all have failed. They may have carved out a sumptuous existence, but to go through life and face death without the *benefit* of having established an early on **"born again" relationship with God the Father through Jesus Christ our Lord and Saviour.** This is the utmost failure and grossest stupidity. **[John 3: 1-8]**, verse 6-7, **"That which is born of the flesh is flesh and tends to death, and that which is born of the Spirit is Spirit, and guarantees life and life more abundantly. Marvel not that I say unto thee,** *Ye must be born again.*"

This **"born again"** relationship with God is without a doubt, the greatest *benefit* a person can enjoy in this lifetime and beyond, for within it are contained all the other **benefits** provided by God. Along with these benefits are the *"rewards"* for **"diligently seeking God"**, **[Hebrews 11:6]**, and **"serving Him with joyfulness and gladness of heart for the abundance of all things"**, **[Deuteronomy 28: 47]**. The vast enrichment and strengthening of this extremely beneficial relationship provides **"great and perfect peace," [Psalms 199: 165; Isaiah 26: 3]**, and **[1 Peter 1: 8]**, **"joy unspeakable and full of glory"** for this life and beyond. This is a very minor introduction to that which awaits the "born again" recipients of the inheritance we have in heaven, including the "New Jerusalem". **[Revelation 21:27]**, **"And there shall in no wise enter into it anything that defileth, neither anything that worketh abomination, or maketh a lie: but they which are written in the Lamb's book of life"**. Let me emphasize here again, the church roster does not qualify as the **Lamb's Book of Life,** never has, never will.

It would be impossible in our finite minds to have a full knowledge of the benefits and rewards that are to be dispensed along the road of life and on into eternity to those willing to meet God's requirements for their reception. We do, however, on a normal basis, possess the mentality to discern the difference between the curses of death and the blessings of life.

Nevertheless, when people are faced with this on a spiritual level, they seem to have a considerable problem deciding to do what is right by God's standards and principles. They may conform to what is deemed as legal by mans thinking and standards, **but will never fit in with God's thoughts and ways, [Isaiah 55: 7-11].** "Ye must be born again"

There is no doubt that if our national leaders, and I use the term "leaders" loosely, had been as ardent in encouraging the populace to study the Bible and follow its teachings as they were in forcing evolution, political correctness, acceptance of whatever erroneous rights one has a tendency to exercise; American's would be much better prepared to make intelligent choices, and our nation would not be suffering the traumas it is experiencing today. **[Proverbs 1: 7], "The fear of the Lord is the beginning of knowledge: but fools** [continue to] **despise wisdom and instruction".**

Any government, including a democracy, regardless of its supposed and claimed superiority, is wholly inadequate to govern without God's guidance and counsel and sooner or later is doomed to failure. History is filled with evidence of this and we haven't learned a thing from it. The signs of this failure are on the horizons even now and drawing closer and becoming more evident each day. **[Matthew 16: 2-3],"**_____**"ye can discern the face of the sky; but can ye not discern the signs of the times".**

It is somewhat amazing, when a person starts a new job they generally like to know what they are going to receive as pay and whatever fringe benefits are available, if any. This is understandable as these things are necessary to our temporal time on this earth. After all it would be nice to be somewhat provided for considering the time and effort on the job. Benefits and rewards become quite important to us as our material needs go on day after day. So we go about finding out all we can about the benefits and rewards of the job, never being sure how long we are going to be around to work it.

Life has no guarantees to it; we never know how many tomorrow's we have left. Then what! So it really becomes very important how we conduct our affairs while we have some control over our life and to know what the rewards, benefits and fringe benefits are for **"living and moving and having our being in Christ; and serving him with joyfulness and gladness of heart for the abundance of all things"**. If we could stretch our minds to know what this *"abundance of all things"* consisted of, we would know what all the rewards, benefits, and benefits were. We are better off not being concerned about it but leaving it up to the Lord to administer at his own discretion. We have our hands full learning, embracing, and initiating the **"better things that accompany salvation, doing always those things that please God"** and have proven ourselves to be utter failures at that. Thank God for his amazing grace.

How we are going to live life depends on what we think about, our thoughts, the content and abundance of our heart and mind, our inner being. **[Luke 6: 45], "A good man out of the good treasure of his heart bringeth forth that which is good; and an evil man out of the evil treasure of his heart bringeth forth that which is evil: for out of the abundance of his heart his mouth speaketh"**.

I have taken the liberty of modifying the last portion of this verse, as follows; **"for out of the abundance of his heart his mind thinketh, his mouth speaketh, and his hand doeth"**. I believe the Edwards rendition of this is in harmony with the rest of the Bible so there is no adding to, nor taking away from the scriptures, but only for the sake of emphasizing it's truth.

There may be a bit of embellishing for understanding sake; I hope it has the desired affect of adding to the **"perfecting of the saints"** and might even be considered as contributing to the **"adorning the doctrine of God", [Titus 2: 10].**

Now that we have considered the monetary and fringe benefits of the job, let's turn our attention to the job itself. What sort of things does this job produce for the good of our society, culture, and nation, indeed the world; or closer to home, maybe you and your family? Or does it in fact produce things that are harmful to our environment, close at hand and far away? Most people, unfortunately don't care as long as they are receiving an adequate paycheck for their services rendered.

Fortunately the majority of jobs is quite favorable in these areas, or at least used to be. However, things are changing in the job market and economic structure of America, not necessarily for the better. There are some things regardless, that are of a detrimental nature with a few even worse than just detrimental, being downright destructive. Still if the pay is good and the profits even better, let those involved, whether employer or employee, beware. These things, though maybe in the minority, are not at all uncommon and abound all around us.

[1 Peter 5: 12], "Be sober, be vigilant, for your adversary the devil, as a roaring lion, walketh about seeking whom he may devour". Rest assured you are his target if you haven't been devoured already. He isn't particular about his victims, for Satan also, is no respecter of persons. He will take the young, the old, the healthy, the infirm; color and condition make no difference. If you are alive, you're his target to devour or to make sure you stay devoured, **[Ephesians 2: 1-3]**. Verse 4, **"But God,** this great magnificent God, steps in to deliver and provide benefits and rewards for those who **[Hebrews 11: 6]**, have faith in him and diligently seek him, his kingdom and his righteousness, [Matthew 6: 33].** Based on this, the benefits and rewards continue for those who avail themselves of his provision to become **"partakers of His divine nature" [1 Peter 1: 3-4].**

Now let us consider the rewards, or penalties, of the rebellious, the disobedient; those listed in **[Romans 1: 18-32]** and mentioned elsewhere as referred to in God's Word. We find reference to this in **[Isaiah 5: 13-14].** Verse 14 gives the reward, **"Therefore hell hath enlarged herself, and opened her mouth without measure: and their glory, and their multitude, and their pomp, and he that rejoiceth, shall descend into it".** This is the sum of their benefits and rewards, or shall we say "results and curses", as "benefits and rewards" have an inference and implication of something good. God from the beginning established himself as the final authority and judge over the affairs of this earth and its inhabitants. Man would be wise to accept this and adjust his thoughts and conduct accordingly.

If those who live in rebellion and disobedience wish to disagree and argue over their final destination, let them take it up with God. It is his word of truth that proclaims this; I am simply proclaiming his word of warning and correction of direction. He has given us his word and essentially said; Here is my Word on the matter, live by obedience to it, or die by disobedience to it, but **DON'T MESS WITH ME.**

[Psalms 2: 1-5]: "Why do the heathen rage and the people imagine a vain thing? The kings of the earth set themselves, and the rulers take counsel together, against the Lord, and against his anointed, saying, Let us break their bands asunder, and cast their cords away from us. He that sitteth in the heavens shall laugh: the Lord shall have them

in derision. Then shall he speak to them in his wrath, and vex them in his sore displeasure".

Many have mistakenly taken God as the kindly old Grandfather type with such love that he would never cast any of his creation into hell. They do not consider that as a God of love; he has to annihilate all which is contrary to the demands of that love. Thus, though he is in fact THE God of love, he is also the God of righteousness, holiness, wrath, and vengeance who hates sin, and as the God of righteousness must destroy all that is opposed to that righteousness, or he ceases to be the God of righteousness and we all lose.

[2 Peter 3: 9; [Acts 26: 20], _____"and then to the Gentiles, that they should repent and turn to God, *and do works meet for repentance"*. **[2 Peter 3; 9], "The Lord is not slack concerning his promise, as some men count slackness, but is longsuffering toward us-ward, not willing that any should perish, but that all should come to repentance". [Mark 1: 14-15],_____"Jesus came into Galilee, preaching the gospel of the kingdom of God, And saying, The time is fulfilled, and the kingdom of God is at hand: repent ye, and believe the gospel".**

God, through Jesus Christ, initiated his own "no child left behind" program a little over 2000 years ago, **[John 3:16], "For God so loved the world that he gave his only begotten Son, that whosoever believeth on Him should not perish, but have everlasting life"**. It didn't originate with President Bush, but God's program hasn't been very successful either, except for the few exceptions, who by their intelligence or simple desperation, turn to God. A *favorable response* to God's provision of salvation is required in order for it to succeed.

Whether by intelligent response to the calling of the Holy Spirit, or by desperation to escape this worldly idiocy with its just consequences; nevertheless **God is faithful to respond and hear their cry of repentance, forgive them of their sin and iniquity, cleansing them of all unrighteousness through the shed blood of Jesus on the cross, and make them free.**

[John 8: 36], "If the son shall make you free, ye shall be free indeed", free to love, serve, and worship God, proclaiming his Word of Truth and Life regardless of the screaming, hollering, whining, and foolishness of the opposers of God and his Word who declare his word to be unconstitutional and a myth. **[Matthew 6: 2],____"Verily I say unto you, they have their reward". [Proverbs 14:1],____"The fool hath said in his heart, there is no God".** Well has our old friend William Shakespeare said, **"What fools ye mortals be".**

Even God's program of salvation and redemption, if it is to be effective, needs appropriate, favorable response to its call and purpose. God's own response to the demands and requirements of his love and commitment to the well being of his creation has always been extremely favorable and beneficial. Unfortunately for man, his response to God's love and devotion has not gone well and shows a terrible lack of intelligence or desire to change. **[Isaiah 55: 7], "Let the wicked forsake his way and the unrighteous man his thoughts, and let him return unto the Lord, and he will have mercy upon him; and to our God, for he will abundantly pardon".**

NOTES

NOTES

VII. INNOCENCE

The Slaughter of the Innocence: This is not in reference to individuals as the innocents that were slaughtered under King Herod's rule in the Bible, but in reference to the condition of "innocence" of the newborn. It seems strange to look at a newborn baby and realize that somewhere within that little child there lurks a monster so evil that it defies understanding. Its origin so far as the human race is concerned began in the Garden of Eden when Adam and Eve first rebelled against God. They abdicated the authority, position, and power, God had given them **[Genesis 1:26]** and submitted it to this monster, Satan. **[Romans 5:12], "Whereby, as by one man sin entered into the world, and death by sin; and so death passed upon all men, for that all have sinned".**

It makes no difference they were deceived, that's the devil's specialty. The fact remains they disobeyed God, invited, and allowed this evil, destructive, monster of sin to become a controlling influence within all humanity that was to follow. As near as we know, Adam and Eve were working under a bit of a handicap without any training or information about this Satan character. All they had was God's command and directions to obey, which should have been sufficient for obedience, but we don't know the extent of what Adam and God talked about while they were together in the Garden. We do know God put Adam in the Garden to dress it and to keep it, **[Genesis 2: 15]**. Verses 16-17 give us a bit more insight into what they talked about including specific directions concerning this tree of the knowledge of good and evil. I'm not to sure that an abundance of information would have made a difference concerning obedience or not; it doesn't seem to have made much difference even since the advent of the Bible and later with the modern abilities to produce such information. Neither has the introduction and continued upgrading and developments of the computer brought on any additional obedience. Whatever could be, and was intended to produce good has immediately been used for evil in a multitude of ways, but such is the mentality and the condition of the heart of man.

We don't know the extent of the information or directions God gave Adam during that time, but whatever it was, Adam blew it big time. We, on the other hand have been given an abundance of knowledge concerning this Satan character and much teaching about his evil ways. We have been given, most of us, considerable time to learn and digest this information, and still it doesn't seem as though we have learned very much. The bulk of humanity while observing their fellows being destroyed by this evil creature continue to follow him and serve him with gusto, and do so while they themselves are being destroyed. There have been piles of books written about this and the process and penalties that are involved in it with the indulgences of sin and iniquity under the influences of this evil one.

Taking the time and doing the study necessary to learn about this destroyer and his evil ways in order to wage an effective warfare against him, is part of the knowledge that is referred to in **[Hosea 4: 6],** that we must have to accumulate and act on to keep from being destroyed. To have all this knowledge at our disposal, but not availing ourselves of it by rejecting or neglecting it, produces a lack of knowledge simply referred to as, "ignorance", which in this situation manifests itself in several different ways. To have it available and not pursue it for the personal knowledge needed is idiotic. To learn it and know it, and not use it to avert destruction is down right stupid. We have all had a run at this, and the vast majority still remain in this position, willingly wallowing in ignorance, idiocy, and stupidity; with Bibles, God's instruction manual for life and life more abundantly all around them, accessible, and still refuse to avail themselves of that which God has made available to them. I do have a tendency to believe mans claims of intelligence are considerably misplaced, unfounded, and exaggerated. Thank God for the exceptions! They are among us providing at least some stability and direction to our nation, society, and culture by their love for God and obedience to his Word.

When this alien invader stakes his claim on a human life would be useless to debate, for we know it doesn't take long for it to manifest itself in some way, possibly as a temper tantrum or some other show of anger. If not taught, trained, disciplined, and guided in the ways of righteousness they will only proceed to get worse. There is no doubt Biblical directives for child rearing have been seriously rejected and neglected, being replaced by a bunch of nonsense conjured up by worldly idiots that have never had a clue on how to raise and teach children. Our present world, and the condition of our children, young people, and those who used to be young, who are now middle aged adults and even older, are living proof of this.

Our nation didn't sink to its degraded condition with the application of God's wisdom, knowledge, understanding, and intelligence. There must be another very apparent reason for its demise; **[Hosea 4: 6], "My people are destroyed or lack of knowledge: because thou hast rejected knowledge, I will also reject thee that thou shalt be no priest to me: seeing thou hast forgotten the law of thy God, I will also forget thy children"**. How would we answer if our young people asked us; why did you forget God and his saving grace and instead, brought destruction down on us? What would your answer be?

The innocence of the babes, the children, the young, and on unto adulthood has been stolen and destroyed by the lack of knowledge of those, who long ago should have known better than to let it happen. And this is still in progress today. **[Hosea 4: 7], "As they were increased, so they sinned against me: therefore will I change their glory into shame"**. And our great, grand, and noble America, because of her embracing of the stupidity and practice of sin, is not as great, grand, and noble as it once was, or as God intended it should be.

This failure in the Biblical directed conditioning of our young, beginning at infancy, is undoubtedly the greatest problem and obstruction our children have in their proper nurturing, growth, and development. The inadvertency involved in neglect of the proper training and teaching of these little ones plus the intentional or unintentional improper influence and conditioning, teaching and training, is what constitutes the "Slaughter of the Innocence", the innocence that these children were born with.

This constitutes the worst form of child abuse ever committed and it is going on right under our noses every day, paid for by your hard earned tax dollars and very likely with some of you unwittingly participating. It would be unconstitutional and illegal for you to do otherwise. Such is the formation of today's laws, rules, and regulations, by our illustrious leaders, forbidding Biblical teaching and implementation in our public arenas, this being done **"by the sleight of men and cunning craftiness, whereby they lie in wait to deceive", [Ephesians 4: 14]**. This also has some serious spiritual implications were contrary religious teachings are allowed while Christianity is being suppressed and insidiously forced and herded into "The Corral of Compliance".

Unfortunately our children were also born with this element of sin deep within them which would surface and manifest itself soon and naturally, much to the chagrin of the parents who naturally thought this little cherub nestled in their arms to be the epitome of perfection.

It is vitally important for parents to realize that this is not a reality of God's doing, and make immediate preparations for the proper God directed training, nurturing, and education of this "little cherub". It will not remain little for long; it will grow and as it grows so will the manifestations of this sinful nature that it was born with that was not apparent to begin with. I realize there are a multitude of variations to be considered here as children differ somewhat from child to child, such differences becoming more apparent and pronounced as they grow older and larger, but all with the common thread of sin running through them that will need to be dealt with, and soon.

With the proper, competent training they at least have a good chance of also growing in spiritual, psychological, stature. This does not take place naturally as does the sinfulness and physical stature, but must be diligently and carefully imposed upon the mentality of this young child with much prayer if this child is to rise above a worldly existence unto a more essential reality of faith, producing an abundant life in Christ.

There are those that considered themselves experts in the rearing of children who have terribly and adversely affected and influenced the psychology of raising children. This has always been a world wide nemesis that can and will only be corrected as mankind submits itself willingly to almighty God, the God of the Bible for correction and direction for their behavior and conduct, included as a foundation for their thinking and thoughts, thus their ways. The condition of your mentality, good or evil, determines your thinking and thoughts, thus your ways and behavior: evil to evil, or good and righteous to good and righteous.

A person lives or exists, depending on their training, by others or self imposed. They live if they have been conditioned in the Biblical art of living and life, otherwise they only exist by default and adversely affect the family, society and culture in which they "exist". It may be a very luxurious existence to be sure, but **without [Deuteronomy 28:47] knowing, gladly and joyfully serving God for the abundance of all things, including health, peace, joy, and soul prosperity,** they have nothing more than a temporary vague existence they misinterpret as life, **[Matthew 16:26] "For what is a man profited, if he should gain the whole world, and lose his own soul? Or what shall a man give in exchange for his soul?"**

Some may say that this venting of anger and sinful tendencies is normal behavior, and I would have to reply, given the fact man has a sinful nature, they are correct. It is this sinful nature that we have to deal with. Its not a matter of bringing it under control but displacing it with the influx of Biblical input and advancing to the position of being a **"Partaker of the divine nature of God", [2 Peter 1: 4], "Whereby are given unto us exceeding great and precious promises: that by these ye might be partakers of the divine nature, having escaped the corruption that is in the world through lust"**. Thus is the sinful nature displaced by obedience to God's word, renewing the mind and diligently keeping the heart, whereby being replaced by the divine nature, **"possessing the vessel with honor", [1 Thessalonians 4: 4]**.

Satan has no mercy, even on the little ones. He is out to destroy by any evil method or way he can devise or invent by way of his followers, **[Romans 1:21-32],** and we are all his targets. But why do people willingly assist him? Certainly a lack of corrective knowledge has much to do with this, the Bible itself providing such knowledge. **[John 10:10] "The thief cometh not, but for to steal, and to kill, and to destroy:**

I am come that they might have life; and that they might have it more abundantly".

The "thief", Satan is out to steal, kill, and destroy your children and he has invented erroneous worldly "child psychology" as a tool to contribute to this, and he has had a lot of assistance in sick minded, erroneous thinking people who willingly assist him in the "Slaughter of the Innocence", especially if they can smell substantial, recognition and profit in it. Our society today is graphic testimony to the failure of this "child psychology" nonsense that was at one time, by the world system, hailed as a real advancement in child rearing. It has however, been instrumental in the destruction of our young and the nation, as the mentality that produced it, and has been produced by it, has continued to mislead and pollute the minds and thinking of all, including those that have become leaders of our nation.

Since this all goes along with, and is an integral part of the sinful nature of man, with all its deception, Satan has been very successful in his mission of destruction, including all those who willingly and blindly serve him and are slaves to his evil, deceitful schemes. Due to sin's unrestricted pleasures, fun, games and momentary self-indulgencies and gratifications, it is pursued and embraced by man in his insatiable appetite for such destructive depravity and conduct. Many of the sinful activities and abominations are described, once again, in **[Romans 1:21-31]. Verse 32** tells a bit more about these people **"Who knowing the judgment of God, that they which commit such things are worthy of death, not only do the same, but have pleasure in them that do them"**. Men always enjoy company in their idiocy, it helps to justify their error and gives encouragement in there own miserable activities.

[Proverbs 22:6] "Train up a child in the way he should go: and when he is old, he will not depart from it." It is to bad that man seems to have to gain most of his wisdom by way of hard knocks and bad experiences when wisdom is available to us through diligent study of the appropriate materials, beginning with God's word as the foundation, inspiration, revelation, and guidance for additional studies. The main problem of gaining wisdom by experiential mans, is that in the time it takes, and due to your own erroneous activities in the interim, you contribute to the destruction of others. There are many ways that a child's innocence is destroyed without them ever knowing or being aware that there is such a death dealing element of destruction within them, or being imposed by some of those they have come to love and trust, just waiting for the opportunity to strike and create its havoc and chaos.

One way is the erroneous instruction and correction they received from their beginning, another is to give no correct instruction at all, to let them find their own way under the constant input of sinful impulses and thinking without Biblical guidance and counsel. If they feed on trash, they will grow go up to be trash cans, and if they are fed trash by trashy leaders, they will experience the same results.

So whose responsibility is it to feed them wholesome, life giving, God directed sustenance? It is indeed the responsibility of all who are in a position of influence, assistance, and care; beginning of course, with their parents. *This expands to include the entire village,* **and certainly the village leaders** of education. However, for the village leaders to become affective in this area, they must become competent in it themselves. America has, however, become terribly lacking in this essential area.

Unfortunately, we live in a world where, in comparison to the multitudes, they are becoming fewer all the time that are qualified in providing the much needed assistance in righteousness and holiness as a foundation for whatever else is needed to provide for life versus existence in this perverted society and world. Our children as well as ourselves are in an ever present danger in this nation that, under the influence and deception of a host of "ne'er do wells", an anti-Christ, anti-Bible, element. There is the constant attempt to excommunicate and expel God from the minds of the people, young and old, thus the borders of our nation. These attempts are, however in vain, but in the meantime they are causing some rather extensive eternal damage to multitudes that are blind enough to follow these blind "leaders" in their pernicious ways. This has brought our America to the point of ruin and our leaders have not had the wisdom, knowledge, courage, and understanding to stop it.

I use the term "leader" here again somewhat loosely as that term should carry something pertaining to at least a shade of nobility and responsibility rather than just being the ramrod of some motley, unsavory, bunch of people that are a detriment to the good of American society as well as each other. I have heard it said that "It takes all kinds of people to make a world". I guess that might have a bit of truth to it if you don't care what kind of world you wind up with, however, my personal opinion is that there are a few "kinds" that we could well do without and have a much better world. God himself will take care of this later as we seem to lack the wherewithal to get the job done.

I wonder if God had this same thought when he ordered the destruction of whole societies and cities such as Sodom and Gomorrah for their whole scale filth and abominations that had contaminated the people. There were other places that fell under the curse of sin and iniquity they brought on themselves. In modern day America these people would have been defended, with their constitutional rights, in spite of how rotten and destructive their lifestyles were to our society. I guess God just doesn't understand constitutional rights, but he sure has a way of straightening things out. Maybe he never heard about relativity, bigotry, diversity, tolerance, etc, etc, in favor of evil. But then maybe he doesn't give a rip about such idiocy, especially when it is such a threat to righteousness, holiness, and common decency according to his standards and values.

[Isaiah 5: 12-14],"_____: but they regard not the work of the Lord, neither consider the operation of his hands. Therefore my people are gone into captivity, because they have no knowledge: and their honourable men are famished, and their multitude dried up with thirst. *"Therefore hell hath enlarged herself, and opened her mouth without measure; and their glory, and their pomp, and he that rejoiceth shall descend into it"*, **[Isaiah 5: 14].**

Along this same line, there are things within each of us that are in need of constant Biblical upgrading and correction in order to make each of us a better person, better people, thus a better world. God himself seems to have this idea in mind in **[Revelation 21]** as he gives us some very pertinent information in **verses 2-3, 23-27,** about "the holy city, new Jerusalem. We also find some interesting and revealing information about the people both inside, and outside of it. **Verses 3-7** concerns those within it, while **verse 8** gives a vivid description of those who are not only outside of it, but possibly not even left on the earth, **"But the fearful, and unbelieving, and the abominable, and murderers, [abortion is included in this, I'm sure God would agree] and whoremongers, and sorcerers, and idolaters, and all liars, shall have their part in the lake** which burneth with fire and brimstone: which is the second death."

Now let's fast forward to **verse 27** where we get some additional information about the inclusion, versus the exclusion of certain "kinds' of people, **"And there shall in no wise [way] enter into it any thing that defileth, neither whatsoever worketh abomination, or maketh a lie: but they which are written in the Lamb's book of life."** [Revelation 22:14] provides another nice bit of information concerning those who are obedient to God's word, **"Blessed are they that do his commandments, that they may have right to the tree of life, and may [have the right to] enter in through he gates of the city"**. Following in **verse 15** we find additional reference to people other than those spoken of in [22:14]. Here's a revelation of information that should prove, at least a little interesting to some people: **church and denominational rosters do not qualify as "The Lambs Book of Life"**.

There are some who may wish to belabor that point; however, it is useless to take it up with me because I am not the one who makes the final judgment on it anyway. Being in agreement or disagreement with me is not important for either of us: however it is vitally important that we both be in agreement with God. He is the umpire in this ballgame of life and to argue over his calls, without repentance, can mean automatic ejection from the ballpark. Just do things his way **[Isaiah 55: 7-9]** to, stay in the game, and "keep your fat out of the fire", so to speak.

It would amaze us if we could at all begin to understand that the horrors and misery, both in this life and in eternity would be alleviated if we would just learn and implement some simple, basic, Biblical principles, and directions for the raising of children. However, what is past is past, we can neither redo nor undo it but we can learn from it, especially if we are not to proud to realize we need some help in our learning processes. Thank God for his mercy, grace, and deliverance that is ours for repenting, and believing the gospel of Jesus Christ unto obedience. Thank God, that because of his great and precious promises, his abundant love and provisions, we can move beyond our mistakes, learn from them, and endeavor to train and teach our children how to avoid the same stupid mistakes we made and possibly will still make from time to time.

It is time for an acknowledgement, realization, and certainly a need for the **[Job 4:21] "Resurrection of the Excellency" which is in them,** an excellency that God designed within man as a part of the image and likeness in which he was created. We must, for our own sake, and for our children's sake, **[Isaiah 64:7] "call upon the name of the Lord and stir up ourselves to take hold of him"** lest we, and our children, be buried alive, forever under our multitudes of iniquities.

[Deuteronomy 30:19], "Therefore choose life that both you and your seed [descendents] may live". We all started out as babes with our innocence, but in spite of the seemingly quiet, peaceful, appearance of these little ones, there is an undercurrent of trouble waiting to manifest itself in due time. This undercurrent of trouble is none other than the **"thief that cometh not but to steal and to kill and destroy",** and whether you will realize it or not, whether you believe it or not, whether you like it or not, he has that little innocent child that he has invaded directly in his sights. He may have already made significant advancements through the body of a drug soaked mother plus other means at his disposal. All the people involved in the process of this abomination of drug addiction would make an interesting study. We see this more as our nation continues in its degradation. How America arrived at this point would make another interesting study.

The only remedy for this disgusting situation is God and his abundant, all sufficient provision of deliverance through Jesus Christ our Saviour and Lord and the constant blending of our lives with this **[John 15: 3]** soul cleansing word that he has spoken unto us. Parents, do you really love and value that sweet little child sleeping peacefully in your arms with all its appearance of apparent innocence? What you see is what God intended, providing conditions are normal as God also intended. **[Proverbs 4:23] "Keep thy heart with all diligence: for out of it are the issues of life".** If you keep your heart with all diligence in submission to God's word you will understand the need to train up this little child in the way it should go, so as it grows it too, will learn how to keep its own heart with all diligence. This is extremely important if you consider that as the issues of life come from the diligently kept heart; so the un-kept heart issues forth death.

In **[Deuteronomy 4:9; 6:6-7; 11:19]** are admonitions and directions as to the teaching and training of children in awareness of the glory and majesty of this great and powerful Jehovah God, creator of heaven and earth and all that is therein. In **[Job 4:20-21]** we find an account of people who have not been taught these things, who have not learned to **"keep their hearts with all diligence". "They are destroyed from morning to evening: they perish forever without any regarding it".** Again in **[Hosea 4:6]: My people are destroyed for lack of knowledge".**

As it was then, so it is today. Our children's innocence is being slaughtered by the lack of proper teaching about God and how he created them and for what purpose. **Verse 6** continues; **"because thou hast rejected knowledge, I will also reject thee, that thou shalt be no priest to me."** Now we have the final, awful result of the failure of parents to obey God in their children's teaching and training, **"seeing thou hast forgotten** the law, WORD, of thy God, I WILL ALSO FORGET THY CHILDREN".

We have some very interesting scripture in **[Matthew 19:13-14], "then were brought unto him, JESUS, little children that he should put his hands on them, and pray: [and the disciples rebuked them.]** It seems that the disciples didn't really learn as they should have from being "in church" about the presence and nature of Jesus and he had to straighten them out once again. Things haven't really changed much in the last 2000 years. The "disciples", even while attending church, still have a difficult time learning, **[Hebrews 5: 11-14.** This sounds a little bit like an introduction to the "separation of church and state" idiocy, but let's go on to **verse 14, "But Jesus said, Suffer the little children, and forbid them not, to come unto me: for of such is the kingdom of heaven."**

Now how are we to bring these little children or any one to the Lord Jesus if it is not through the avenue of his WORD, his truth, his counsel? This has become more difficult with the invasion of "the separation of church and state" which has tended to plug the conduit of God's word, the church, with erroneous laws, rules, and regulations. How are we going to keep the word flowing if we have not set ourselves to get prepared to do so? Do you take your own in-depth study of God's word serious, or do you even have any **in-depth study, delighting, and meditation of his word, [Psalms 1:2]?** Do you perceive enough value in it for the direction of your entire family in the instruction of righteousness unto salvation, redemption, and reconciliation with God? Or do you just settle for enough of it to be comfortable in your local church, without any depth or spiritual substance required?

We older ones are not released from the responsibility of instruction just because our children have left home and have their own children. In **[Deuteronomy 4:9],** the last part of the verse in reference to Biblical teaching says, **"but teach them to thy sons,** *and to thy sons' sons".* These are your grandchildren, just in case you didn't pick up on that. Grandpa, grandma, you are not off the hook when it comes to teaching your "family". Had the innocence of so many children not been slaughtered in the last fifty to seventy years by rejecting, and neglecting of God's instructions about the proper teaching of our young we wouldn't be having the problems to the extent we are having them today.

One of the great problems we are seeing all around us; there are many, are grandparents raising their grandchildren because their own children do not have what it takes to fulfill the responsibilities of raising these children themselves as God intended. Instead we stood aside and allowed the **"whole counsel of God" to be replaced by the substitution of trash and garbage by some so called child psychology experts educated in "the evil inventions" of worldly wisdom of man's devising and idiocy, [Ephesians 4: 14].** We have in our ignorance and, in total indifference to God's word, **"given place to the devil", [Ephesians 4:27], "That we be no more children, tossed to and fro, and carried about with every wind of doctrine, by the sleight of men, and cunning craftiness, whereby they lie in wait to deceive".** We can see the results in the nations children today, including our world and nation, though the gradual and insidious deception, of our, **[Hosea 4:6], "forgetting, rejecting, and neglecting, the word of our God".**

Thank God for the exceptions who remembered God's instructions, and have nurtured their little ones in the counsel of the Lord. I must confess, I have not done well in this area and my children have paid the price for their father's failure to gather them around the kitchen table and teach them about this great, wonderful, loving God and his son Jesus, our redeemer. I just took them to Sunday School and Church like I was taught to do and left it all up to the pastors and Sunday School teachers. I was to realize, as the years went by, that most of these dear well meaning saints were no more qualified than I was to teach these spiritual truths. We can be very thankful for God's amazing grace.

I never really knew the principles spelled out in **Deuteronomy chapters 4, 6, and 11,** mentioned earlier until I got involved in this study at home. By then my own children were grown and gone without some vital essentials of Biblical truths and principles that I, as their father, should have taught them that they needed to know to raise their own families.

Listen to me you young parents with your little ones. By all means, take your family to Sunday School and Church but, do not neglect to teach them diligently at home about this great God of heaven and his abundant goodness that leads men to repentance. Teach them the need of keeping their hearts with all diligence, teach them of the need for soul depth repentance, a cleaning out of the garbage of sin from their lives and souls, to be displaced and replaced by the knowledge and practice "the doing" of God's Word, the input of love, forgiveness, mercy, and the amazing grace of God through Jesus Christ unto life and life more abundantly. Show them and teach them the process of displacing and crowding out of the things of evil and destruction by study and input of the **"things that [John 8:29] always please God, and the things that [Hebrews 6:9] accompany salvation". A good place to start is [Galatians 5:22-23], the "fruit of the Spirit."**

Don't just learn these "things" for the purpose of memorization; but practice them with diligence to make them characteristic of your lifestyle, otherwise they will do you no good. There are others to be included and could well be considered also as fruit of the Spirit, such as forgiveness and patience, and the list continues to the gaining of wisdom, understanding, knowledge, and the development of intelligence for the continued enrichment and enhancement of your life and the lives of your children. May God bless and guide you in your endeavors as you stir up yourself, and your children, to take hold of him and **"do always those things that, please him"**, **"initiating those better things that accompany salvation"**, [John 8: 29; Hebrews 6: 9].

NOTES

VIII. BEFORE COFFEE THOUGHTS

A government that does not tend to the security and overall well-being, the good, of its subjects, is not worthy, nor qualified to even being thought of as "government", and is a detriment and obstacle to the securing of such security and well-being of all, including itself. Any system or government that is guilty of such transgressions places itself, its subjects, and the nation, country, or land, it is intended to serve and protect, into a self-destruct mode.

It may well take some time, and generally does where sin abounds, even when God's grace is present: but rest assured sin will collect its dues and **"the wages of sin is still death", [Romans 6:23].** Sin always has, and still does, carry its own retribution. This has not changed and applies to any and every entity from an individual to, and including a nation, and indeed, the world.

The establishment and promotion of well-being and the **"goodness of God" [Romans 2:4],** is without a doubt God's will, for such a government will establish and encourage Biblical principles for not only the glory of God, but for the spiritual benefits of all as well as the physical and material, the temporal needs and benefits that are required for life and living. **[2 Peter 3:9] "For God is not willing that any should perish, but is willing, that all should come to repentance, and [Mark 1:15] believe the gospel",** certainly unto obedience.

When we learn to want for ourselves, understanding that this is what we need, what God wants for us, then our species will begin to advance in the things that are of most benefit to all, including and most important of all, God's pleasure. For until we have learned the essence of **[Revelation 4:11]**, we have learned nothing at all; government has learned nothing at all and as a result, in its ignorance of Biblical knowledge and truth, is unable to lead the people in the ways of righteousness, **nor does it have the presence of mind to even encourage them to pursue the ways of righteousness.** *Consequently, all is lost with the exceptions of those individuals whose government is the Lord, his word of truth is their constitutional law, and his abiding Holy Spirit is their divine nature.*

We would be living in, and enjoying a different and an exceedingly more wonderful nation today if the government of the people, by the people, and for the people were disposed to such conditions as that. However, it is not and we are not. As a result, even the exceptions are adversely affected by the prevailing, anti-Bible, anti-God tendencies of the "authorities" that bear rule, **[Proverbs 14:34; 28:9; 29:2]**.

These adversities, which are characteristic of the "gates of hell", though they try, do not prevail against these exceptions that **constitute the church that Jesus is building, [Matthew 16:18].** Within *this church* there is a government that is dedicated and committed to the advancement of **[John 8:29], "those things that always please God", [2 Corinthians 10:5] casting down "vain" imaginations and every high thing that exalteth itself against the knowledge of God,** including erroneous government, **and bringing into captivity every thought to the obedience of Christ, resulting [Isaiah 55:8-9], in our thoughts conforming to God's thoughts and our ways conforming to his ways.**

We have a world full, and churches full of people that need this desperately. **Even the "exceptions" need an occasional [John 15:3], "spiritual tune-up" along these lines from time to time to remain on that [Matthew 7:14], "narrow way". [1 Peter 4:17-18] "For the time is come that judgment must**

begin at the house of God: and if it first begin at us, what shall the end be of them that obey not the gospel of God? And if the righteous scarcely be saved, where shall the ungodly and the sinner appear"? As enjoyable as this journey is in the presence of God we are not home yet, therefore, **[Proverbs 4:23], "Keep thy heart with all diligence, for out of it are the issues of life".**

The other side of the coin is, out of the un-kept, unguarded, non-Bible "life", God's Word, conditioned heart, flow the issues of sin and its wages, death. These "retributive" wages of sin are always hiding in the shadows of stupidity waiting to pounce on the ignorant and foolish; those who refuse to learn their lessons concerning previous transgressions well. **[Galatians 6:7-8] "Be not deceived: God is not mocked: for whatsoever a man soweth, that shall he [and his seed], also reap. For he that soweth to his flesh shall of the flesh reap corruption; but he that soweth to the Spirit shall of the Spirit reap life everlasting".**

This also may well be passed on to his "seed". It would do well for Fathers to pay close attention to this principle found in **[Deuteronomy 30:19] & [Hosea 4:6] and implement the principles found in [Deuteronomy 4:9; 6:7; 18:19] concerning the teaching and conditioning of your children in the Lord and his majesty.** *We live in a nation, indeed a world, where this is not being done, and we, our children, and our children's children, are paying a horrible price for this transgression.* One of the main contributing factors concerning grandparents now raising their grandchildren is the fact that these, now grandparents, failed in their responsibilities in raising their own children according to Bible principles to be Bible practicing parents that they could pass on to their children. There certainly are exceptions to this, some beyond our control, but it is hoped America will learn from these experiences.

America has sown to the flesh and of the flesh is reaping its just "wages" and our government is not even encouraging a repentance; but repentance as a Bible and church principle and command, is blocked by the implementation of an idiotic "separation of church and state" concept. **[Deuteronomy 10:12-13], "And now, America,** *State and Church inclusive,* **what doth the Lord thy God require of thee, but to fear the Lord thy God, to walk in all his ways, and to love him, and to serve the Lord thy God with all thy heart and with all thy soul, To keep the commandments of the Lord, and his statutes, which I command thee this day for thy good"?** The principles neither diminish nor die. They are always in force. You will either live by obedience to them or die by your disobedience to them. This is also a principle that is reinforced throughout God's Word, page by page, cover to cover.

Like it or not, it is God's legislation of righteousness. Accept it, love it, enjoy it, and live; Reject it, neglect it, despise it, and die; it is as simple as that.

I realize that doesn't sound very loving and kind, but we must understand that God is love, kindness, goodness, righteousness, holiness, purity, etc, etc; just to touch on a few of the things that are descriptive of his divine nature. His principles must be observed to produce their results. This is what he is and it is impossible for him to be otherwise. He must, to remain who and what he is, maintain and promote his divine nature in all he possesses, including humanity, or he ceases to be who and what he is and we are all lost forever.

He is so beyond our ability to understand all this, so to attempt to "prove that God exists" is absolute foolishness, but is light of all that is visible and proof of what is invisible. It takes much less faith to believe that he is, than it takes to believe in something otherwise; which because it is otherwise and does therefore not exist as a viable option, can offer no manifestation or proof of itself. **[Hebrews 11:6], "But without faith it is impossible to please him, which is our purpose for being; for he that cometh to God must believe that he is, and that he is a rewarder of them that diligently seek him";** devoting and committing themselves to the same ends and results that God himself has devoted and committed himself to, the promotion of absolute righteousness.

[Matthew 6:33], "But seek ye first, and above all, the kingdom of God, and HIS RIGHTEOUSNESS, and all these things, wisdom, understanding, knowledge, common sense, intelligence, etc., will be added unto you". It will be immediately obvious to a student of God's word that I have added a few things in the quotations that are specifics within the context of the contents of God's kingdom, righteousness, and his divine nature, but which are in no way a complete list of what is to be found there. A continuation of these things may be found in **[Galatians 5: 22-23]** as well as throughout other portions of God word of absolutes and truth.

I would invite you, saved and unsaved alike, to search, explore, and discover for yourselves the vast treasures of life and life more abundantly **[John 10:10],** that are to found there. It will give us all something extremely constructive and beneficial to do, and do together for the rest of our lives. To simply receive inspiration by writing of these things is a treasure to be joyously experienced in itself. **This [Romans 12: 2] renewing of your mind admonition really pays off.** Try it; you'll like it, though you might find it a bit difficult at first.

God being who he is, and God being what he is, opposition to him, his will, his desires, his pleasure, his happiness, etc., is something that, based on wisdom and mans own well being, just is not done nor even contemplated. Unfortunately, wisdom is quite lacking in this area, consequently consideration of God and his multiple benefits and rewards are also quite lacking. It's kind of like running red lights; you may get away with it for awhile, but until the practice of the violation of the law is repented of and stopped, you will pay dearly for your transgression as will others that are immediately adjacent to, and so affected by your stupidity.

The intent and purpose of the law is to keep and maintain the safety of those who are in need of obedience of the law. Other people, drivers and passengers in other vehicles as well as passengers in your own vehicle, or pedestrians, who are in close proximity to you, all fall in the category of those who are within your sphere of influence, whether or not you are possessing your vehicle, your vessel, with sanctification and honor. Those, who by their nature, personality, practice correct manner of living, and doing always those things contained within the law, need those who are not so disposed, to be subject to the law and obedience to it for the safety of us all. In this way, a certain condition of unity, harmony, safety, and well being of all is established and maintained.

However, if there are those present who obey the law simply because it is demanded, but whose nature is not commensurate with the law and opposed to its intention and purpose, rest assured there will be transgressions, and the tranquility and pleasure of the society where this transgression takes place will be disrupted, people will be destroyed, and God will not be pleased. This places everyone in a very precarious position; both those who commit the transgressions and those who are disposed to allow and tolerate such transgressions and offering little or no opposition for correction to such erroneous behavior and conduct which places them in a position of aiding and abetting such transgressions. Government, including democracy is supposed to be the solution to this dilemma, but cause more problems than they solve. God never intended government to oppose him and his righteousness, but be in harmony with him in maintaining "decency and order. **[1 Corinthians 14: 40], "Let ALL THINGS be done decently and in order"** according to Bible directed counsel which includes the duties, functions, operation, and responsibilities of government. **[Proverbs 29: 2], "When the righteous are in authority, the people rejoice: but when the wicked beareth rule, the people mourn"**.

This reveals a deceptive segment within the whole community whose deception in concern of obedience to the law was always there, concealed and waiting for an opportunity to strike, but not necessarily apparent or visible by what they said, how they lived, or the position or place in the community they held. Unfortunately our world, nations, individuals, and societies have been, it seems, quite adversely affected by these "deceptive individuals" and the groups they form.

We who live in America have inadvertently been conned into providing these individuals and groups a certain protection under a misused and abused; by other deceptive individuals and groups, a constitution that allows, thus encouraging, promoting and safeguarding, the continuing practices of transgressions. These things are no longer hidden, but the deceptions, transgressions, and overall attitudes, personalities, and contrary natures that produce them are blatantly spitting in the face of all society and God himself, and all this is protected under "constitutional rights" to do so.

It is amazing how degraded and ridiculous a society can become when they **"professing themselves to be wise have become fools",[Romans 1: 22],** and have elevated the inferior laws of man with his lack of Godly wisdom, understanding, knowledge, intelligence, and plain old common sense to prevail, and those who make them, to become god in the land **while God and his word have been cast aside and despised.**

The deceptive manipulation, use, and abuse of such power that has been placed in the hands of incompetent ruling authorities, have contributed greatly and terribly to the downfall of America. **[Psalms 111:10] [Proverbs 1:7; 4:7; 9:10]:** Biblical and Godly, wisdom, knowledge, understanding, intelligence and common sense have been **"cast away and despised",[Isaiah 5:24],** thrown to the wind and replaced with "political correctness", diversity, acceptance, toleration, relativity, if it feels good do it, excess, and transgressions; and the lack of knowledge and ignorance goes on and on to the ultimate destruction of all participants and proponents, who because of their being proponents are also participants. These, who in their devious lifestyles of treachery are revealed and described in **[Romans 1:32], "Who knowing the judgment of God, that they which commit such things are worthy of death, not only do the same, but have pleasure in them that do them".**

NOTES

NOTES

NOTES

NOTES